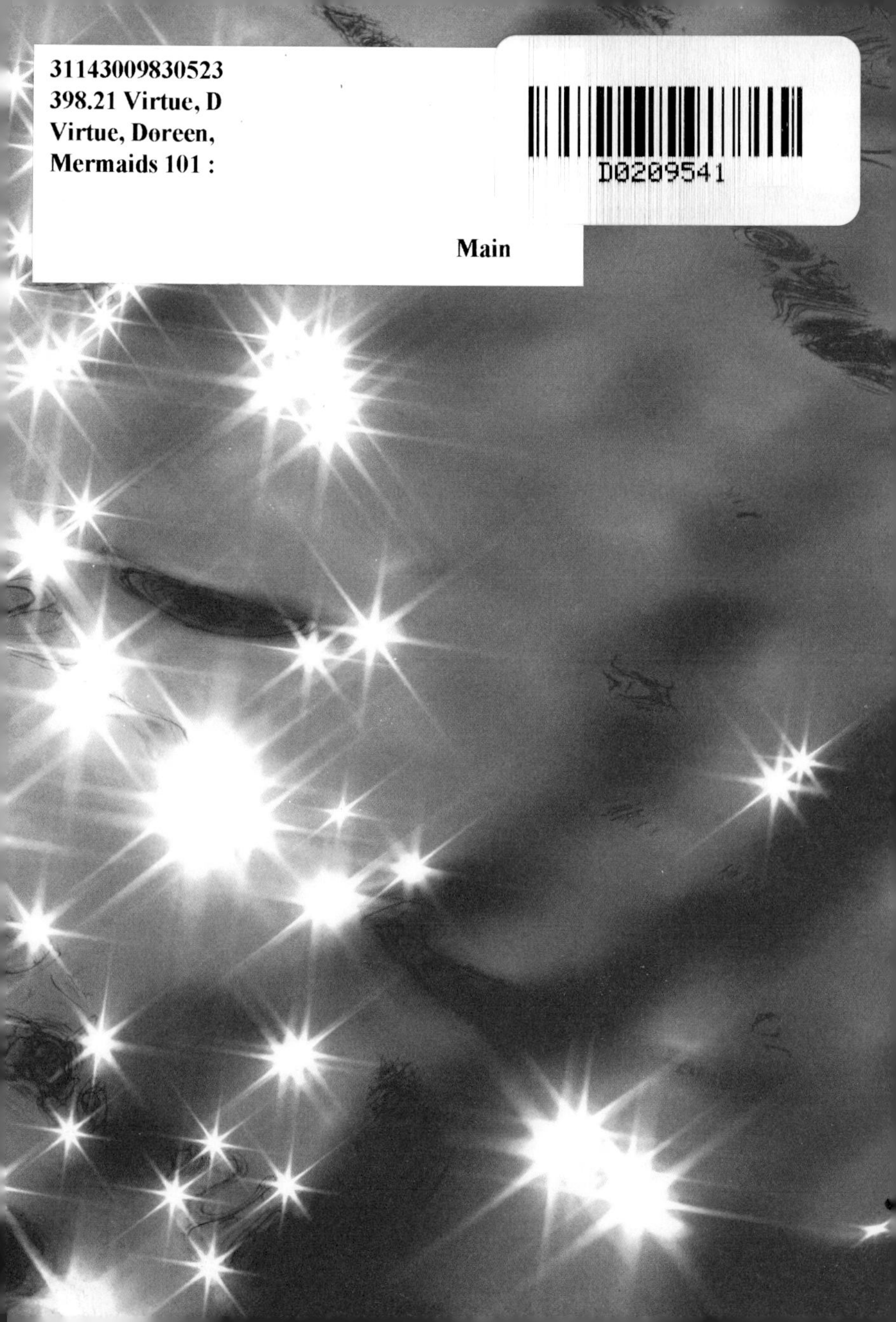

MERMAIDS 101

Also by Doreen Virtue

Books/Kits/Oracle Board

Assertiveness for Earth Angels (available July 2013)
The Miracles of Archangel Gabriel (available March 2013)
Flower Therapy (with Robert Reeves)
Mary, Queen of Angels
Saved by an Angel
The Angel Therapy® Handbook
Angel Words (with Grant Virtue)
Archangels 101
The Healing Miracles of Archangel Raphael
The Art of Raw Living Food (with Jenny Ross)
Signs from Above (with Charles Virtue)
The Miracles of Archangel Michael
Angel Numbers 101
Solomon's Angels (a novel)
My Guardian Angel (with Amy Oscar)
Angel Blessings Candle Kit (with Grant Virtue; includes booklet, CD, journal, etc.)
Thank You, Angels! (children's book with Kristina Tracy)
Healing Words from the Angels
How to Hear Your Angels
Realms of the Earth Angels
Fairies 101
Daily Guidance from Your Angels
Divine Magic
How to Give an Angel Card Reading Kit
Angels 101
Angel Guidance Board
Goddesses & Angels
Crystal Therapy (with Judith Lukomski)
Connecting with Your Angels Kit (includes booklet, CD, journal, etc.)
Angel Medicine
The Crystal Children
Archangels & Ascended Masters
Earth Angels
Messages from Your Angels
Angel Visions II
Eating in the Light (with Becky Prelitz, M.F.T., R.D.)
The Care and Feeding of Indigo Children
Healing with the Fairies
Angel Visions
Divine Prescriptions
Healing with the Angels
"I'd Change My Life If I Had More Time"
Divine Guidance
Chakra Clearing
Angel Therapy®
The Lightworker's Way
Constant Craving A–Z
Constant Craving
The Yo-Yo Diet Syndrome
Losing Your Pounds of Pain

Audio/CD Programs
The Healing Miracles of Archangel Raphael
Angel Therapy® Meditations
Archangels 101 (abridged audio book)
Fairies 101 (abridged audio book)
Goddesses & Angels (abridged audio book)
Angel Medicine (available as both 1- and 2-CD sets)
Angels among Us (with Michael Toms)
Messages from Your Angels (abridged audio book)
Past-Life Regression with the Angels
Divine Prescriptions
The Romance Angels
Connecting with Your Angels
Manifesting with the Angels
Karma Releasing
Healing Your Appetite, Healing Your Life
Healing with the Angels
Divine Guidance
Chakra Clearing

DVD Program
How to Give an Angel Card Reading

Oracle Cards (divination cards and guidebook)
Indigo Angel Oracle Cards (with Charles Virtue; available July 2013)
Angel Dreams Oracle Cards (with Melissa Virtue; available March 2013)
Mary, Queen of Angels Oracle Cards
Angel Tarot Cards (with Radleigh Valentine and Steve A. Roberts)
The Romance Angels Oracle Cards
Life Purpose Oracle Cards
Archangel Raphael Healing Oracle Cards
Archangel Michael Oracle Cards
Angel Therapy® Oracle Cards
Magical Messages from the Fairies Oracle Cards
Ascended Masters Oracle Cards
Daily Guidance from Your Angels Oracle Cards
Saints & Angels Oracle Cards
Magical Unicorns Oracle Cards
Goddess Guidance Oracle Cards
Archangel Oracle Cards
Magical Mermaids and Dolphins Oracle Cards
Messages from Your Angels Oracle Cards
Healing with the Fairies Oracle Cards
Healing with the Angels Oracle Cards

All of the above are available at your local
bookstore, or may be ordered by visiting:

Hay House USA: **www.hayhouse.com**®
Hay House Australia: **www.hayhouse.com.au**
Hay House UK: **www.hayhouse.co.uk**
Hay House South Africa: **www.hayhouse.co.za**
Hay House India: **www.hayhouseco.in**

Doreen's website: **www.AngelTherapy.com**

MERMAIDS 101

Exploring the Magical Underwater
World of the Merpeople

DOREEN VIRTUE

HAY HOUSE, INC.

Carlsbad, California • New York City
London • Sydney • Johannesburg
Vancouver • Hong Kong • New Delhi

Published and distributed in the United States by: Hay House, Inc.: www.hayhouse.com® • *Published and distributed in Australia by:* Hay House Australia Pty. Ltd.: www.hayhouse.com.au • *Published and distributed in the United Kingdom by:* Hay House UK, Ltd.: www.hayhouse.co.uk • *Published and distributed in the Republic of South Africa by:* Hay House SA (Pty), Ltd.: www.hayhouse.co.za • *Distributed in Canada by:* Raincoast: www.raincoast.com • *Published in India by:* Hay House Publishers India: www.hayhouse.co.in

Cover design: Julie Davison • *Interior design:* Tricia Breidenthal

Library of Congress Cataloging-in-Publication Data

Virtue, Doreen.
  Mermaids 101 : exploring the magical underwater world of the merpeople / Doreen Virtue.
    p. cm.
  ISBN 978-1-4019-3884-0 (hardcover : alk. paper)
  1. Mermaids. I. Title.
  GR910.V57 2012
  398.21--dc23

                        2012021735

Hardcover ISBN: 978-1-4019-3884-0
Digital ISBN: 978-1-4019-3886-4

15 14 13 12   4 3 2 1
1st edition, November 2012

Printed in China

To the whales,
the dolphins,
and the water,
with love,
respect, and
gratitude.

Contents

Introduction

REAL MERMAIDS

Our planet is over 70 percent water, containing an estimated 332.5 million cubic miles of water. Given this volume, is it inconceivable to imagine that there are aquatic creatures beyond our comprehension? After all, as researchers dive deeper in the oceans, each year they discover new species of fish, shark, crab, and other sea dwellers.

Mermaids and mermen are one-half human and one-half fish. Their upper bodies look human from the torso to the head, while from the stomach down they sport fish scales, fins, and tails. They can

$\mathcal{M}$ERMAIDS INHABIT OUR
OCEANS AND LAKES, AND
CAN BE SEEN BY THOSE WITH
OPEN MINDS AND HEARTS.

breathe and see clearly underwater without diving equipment.

Different varieties include:

- **Merangels:** These mermaids and mermen have a celestial connection, and are compelled to help save the ocean and its inhabitants.

- **Merfairies:** Mermaids and mermen who guard bodies of freshwater and their inhabitants, Merfairies are thinner and more petite than Merangels.

- **Selkies:** These mermaids appear as seals while in the ocean and as female humans while on land. They're most commonly found in Scotland. In Ireland, they're called Roanes. Selkies help fishermen and sailors.

- **Undines:** These "sea sprites," derived from Greek figures known as *Nereids,* are tiny, light-colored, wingless beings who govern and live in water. You can see and hear them playing in the spray of the ocean. (*Sirens,* another category

of creatures from Greek mythology that are often confused with mermaids, are human females with bird features, including talons instead of feet. They are infamous for singing irresistibly seductive songs to sailors, and then fatally luring them deep into the ocean.)

Ask a little girl (of any age!) if she loves mermaids, and you'll be met with squeals and smiles. Many girls emulate mermaids in the swimming pool, especially these days, with the proliferation of "swimmable" mermaid tails (more information on this topic can be found in Chapter 7).

Do mermaids really exist, or are they products of sailors' delusions from too many days at sea? Legends say that mariners, lonely for female companionship, mistook manatees and dolphins for mermaids. I believe that mermaids, unicorns, fairies, and other so-called mythical animals once lived as physical beings on Earth. After all, these creatures are represented in countless paintings, carvings, and writings around the world since ancient times. They were either hunted into extinction, or they elected to move

S WIMMABLE MERMAID
TAILS ALLOW US
TO EXPERIENCE
THE MAGIC OF
MERMAIDING.

to a higher-vibrational frequency (nonphysical) that only pure-hearted believers can access.

The word *mermaid* comes from the Old English word *mere,* which means "sea" or "lake," and *maid,* which means "girl" or "woman." Mermaids are an internationally recognized archetype, called by many names:

- *Deniz kızı* in Turkey
- *Havfrue* in Denmark
- *Iara* in Brazil
- *Meerfrau* and *Wassernixe* in Germany
- *Merrow, muirruhgach,* or *selkie* in Ireland and Scotland
- *Merrymaid* in Cornwall
- *Oceanid, Nereid,* and *Naiad* in Greece
- *Rusalka* in Slavic countries
- *Sirena* in Italy, Spain, and the Philippines
- *Sirène* in France
- *Sjöjungfru* in Sweden

A search of world language dictionaries shows interesting meanings of the root *mer* and its derivatives *mar, mara,* and *mir.* The words for "mother" and "sea" are related in French (*mère* and *mer*), German (*Mutter* and *Meer*), Italian (*madre* and *mare*), and Spanish (*madre* and *mar*). The linguistic link between sea and mother seems to be one more reference to our ancient roots to the ocean. Are the Merpeople our ancestors? This is a topic we'll explore throughout this book, particularly in Chapter 2.

Mermaids 101 continues my *101* series exploring the otherworldly, which includes the books *Angels 101, Archangels 101*, and *Fairies 101*. ("101" is a term used in college courses to signify an introductory class.) In this book, as with the others in the series, we'll explore the history of these magical beings, as well as their connection to our daily lives. Some of the material in these pages is extracted from my other works in an effort to make sure that this is a thorough overview of the mermaid realm.

You may be wondering, *Are mermaids as real as angels and fairies?* From the information in this book, I hope you'll draw your own conclusions. Although

MERMAIDS APPEAR IN ART-WORK AND STATUES AROUND THE GLOBE, SUCH AS THIS ONE AT THE FOUNTAIN OF NEPTUNE AT THE PLAZA NAVONA IN ROME.

mermaids are considered beautiful fantasy images, you may decide that they're something more. Perhaps, like unicorns, mermaids once physically existed upon this earth but became extinct or ascended to the nonphysical level to escape painful exploitation. Could this be why so many ancient paintings depict both unicorns and mermaids?

Like me, you may be naturally drawn to paintings and stories about mermaids, and find pleasure in looking at their images. Mermaids, after all, represent powerful and independent beings who live adventurous nature-based lives. Perhaps this is why this archetype intrigues men and women alike.

While mermen occasionally appear in art and the media, merfolk generally are female. They're related to "water goddesses," which include the Blessed Mother Mary, the Hindu deity Lakshmi, the Buddhist bodhisattva Quan Yin, the Inuit deity Sedna, and the African and Brazilian goddess Yemanja.

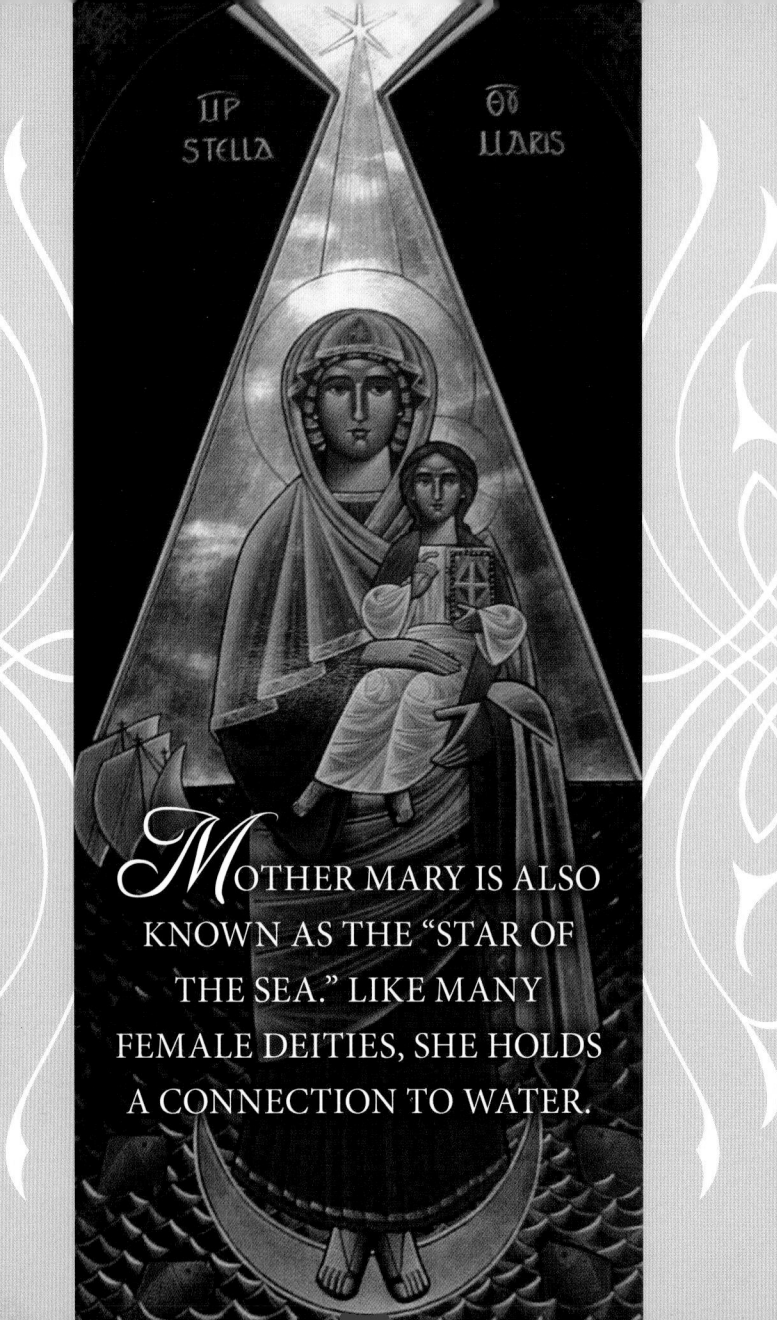

MOTHER MARY IS ALSO KNOWN AS THE "STAR OF THE SEA." LIKE MANY FEMALE DEITIES, SHE HOLDS A CONNECTION TO WATER.

Images of mermaids date back to ancient Babylonian times. As you'll read in this book, the cultural references to fish gods and goddesses hold clues to the mysteries of Atlantis and our connection to Sirius and other star systems.

Hans Christian Andersen's iconic fairy tale "The Little Mermaid" has been reworked and popularized by Disney's cartoon and amusement-park ride of the same name. Our modern world continues to pay homage to mermaids in movies (for example, *Splash, Aquamarine,* and *Pirates of the Caribbean: On Stranger Tides*); television programs (*H2O: Just Add Water* from Australia, for instance); and in business logos (most notably, Starbucks Coffee Company).

One thing's for sure: the image of mermaids is embedded within our culture, lending a magical tone and harking back to ancient times. In Chapter 1, we'll explore the ancient spiritual beliefs connected to merfolk.

$$\textit{\$ \$ \$}$$

CHAPTER ONE

MER-DEITIES

Many ancient gods and goddesses looked like mermen and mermaids. There are deities and creation legends worldwide associated with the sea, many of which include figures of mermaids and mermen. Many cultures believe that life originated in the ocean, born of fishlike creators. These fish deities taught the local humans important new skills, such as farming and horticulture.

Fish Deities

Some deities have fish tails, including:

- The first recorded mermaid goddess was **Atargatis** from the Syrian culture.

- The first recorded merman god was **Ea** or **Oannes** in Babylon, who reportedly brought civilization, including writing and science, to humans.

- **Dagon**, the merman fertility god of Babylon, taught humans how to grow, plow, and harvest grain (his name means "grain"). In fact, Dagon's temple and image are spoken of in the Bible in 1 Samuel 5: 2–7.

DAGON, THE BABYLONIAN MERMAN GOD OF GRAIN, WAS WRITTEN ABOUT IN THE BIBLE.

✴ The Chinese creator deities, **Fu Hsi** and **Nü Kua**, are a merman and mermaid, respectively.

✴ In India, the **Nagas** are beautiful half humans with coiled lower bodies who live in the sea. Most have the head and upper torso of a woman, with a long green tail that could be that of a dragon, snake, or fish.

✴ In Maori and Polynesian cultures, **Ikatere** is the fish god who fathered all sea beings, including mermaids.

✴ In Africa, **Mami Wata** is a fish-tailed water goddess frequently portrayed holding a serpent (which is also a symbol connected with water).

✴ The Egyptian deities **Isis** and **Osiris** are often depicted with fish on their heads, or with fish tails.

SIS IS FREQUENTLY PORTRAYED WITH A FISH ON HER HEAD OR A FISH TAIL.

- Vishnu, the primary Hindu deity, first incarnated as **Matsya**, a merman who saved the world from a great flood and preserved the Vedas (sacred texts).

Water Deities

Some water gods and goddesses have humanlike (instead of merfolk-like) bodies. These deities are associated with the water, but don't necessarily live in it:

- **Lakshmi,** the Hindu goddess of abundance, who sits atop a lotus, is companion to Ganesh and Vishnu, two male deities who are also associated with water.

- **Sarasvati** is the Hindu river goddess of music, science, the arts, and knowledge.

- **Quan Yin** is the Buddhist bodhisattva of compassion.

*Q*UAN YIN IS THE BUDDHIST
WATER GODDESS OF COMPASSION.

5

- **Sedna** is the Inuit goddess who supplies an abundant harvest from the sea.

- **Yemanja**, the African and Brazilian mother goddess, is a protector and nurturer.

- The name of the Celtic goddess **Danu**, or Dana, means "Waters from Heaven." Many rivers are named for her, including the Danube, Dnieper, Dniester, and Don. Sacred wells and rivers are considered entryways to the Divine Mother, and Dana was a mother creator goddess.

- One of **Jesus Christ**'s symbols is a fish. Some people believe that this sign is associated with Christianity, and Jesus himself is a symbol of our watery origins (in addition to Christ's miracle of multiplying fishes and loaves).

- **Venus** or **Aphrodite** is the Greco-Roman love goddess who was born from the foam of the sea.

$\mathcal{V}$ENUS OR APHRODITE IS THE
GRECO-ROMAN LOVE GODDESS
WHO ORIGINATED FROM THE SEA.

Now that we've touched upon this veneration of water deities and the creation stories of fish gods who brought civilization to Earth, it's time to examine the question of our watery origins as a human species. Perhaps we're all merfolk, as we'll explore in the next chapter.

CHAPTER TWO

DID WE ALL ORIGINATE AS MERPEOPLE?

All humans share mitochondrial DNA—a kind of genetic material that is passed down without recombination—which can be traced to one woman who lived between 170,000 and 200,000 years ago. Scientists nicknamed this woman "Mitochondrial Eve," and their studies show that people from varied races and cultures all share her as the most recent matrilineal common ancestor. Her mitochondrial DNA has been passed down through everyone's mothers,

Did we all originate from the sea?

since the mitochondrial genome is inherited only through women. Further research is confirming this finding, and has pinpointed Mitochondrial Eve's geographic location as East Africa.

In fact, paleoanthropologists have an "out of Africa" theory to account for our origins. They believe that the patrilineal most recent common ancestor, a 60,000- to 140,000-year-old male dubbed "Y-Chromosomal Adam," also came from Africa. Some theorists believe that early human ancestors waded along the sea, eating fish and sea plants. This watery existence no doubt spurred the need for an aquatic body.

From the Stars

I believe there's a connection between Mitochondrial Eve and Y-Chromosomal Adam's genesis in Africa and the creation legends of the West African Dogon tribe. The Dogon have long shared stories identifying a planet circling the star Sirius as the origin of humanity. In their legends, the Dogon say that the original humans were amphibians with fish tails, who landed on Earth in a vessel accompanied by fire and thunder. Additionally, this tribe's name is similar to that of the Babylonian fish deity

Dagon. As you'll recall from the previous chapter, Dagon is the merman god who taught humans how to cultivate grain.

The Dogon tribe are "off the grid" and disconnected from modern technology and media. For a few decades, starting in 1931, they were studied by anthropologists, who heard Dogon priests explain the legends of fishlike gods from Sirius. According to them, the tribe was visited by a group of fish-tailed people called the Nommos who came from the star next to Sirius. This amphibious race of beings, half human and half fish, came to Earth and created bodies of water. They then taught the Africans how to fish and how to drink water (*Nommos* means "to make one drink").

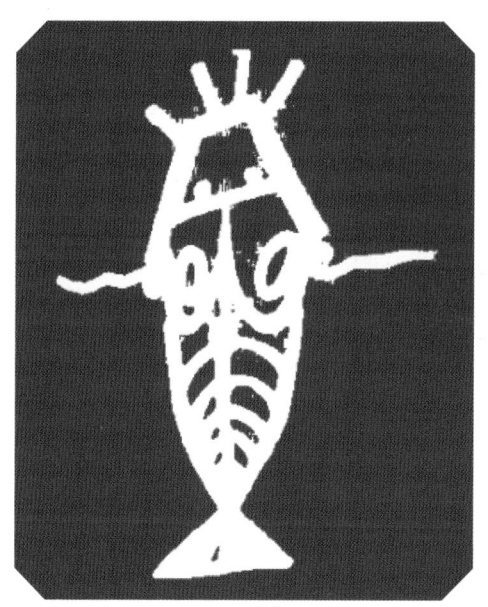

$\mathcal{T}$HE DOGON AFRICAN TRIBE SAY
THAT THEY WERE VISITED BY FISH
GODS FROM SIRIUS, WHICH THEY'VE
DEPICTED IN THESE DRAWINGS.

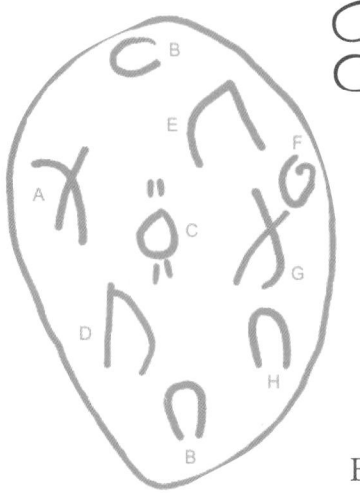

*T*HE AFRICAN DOGON TRIBE'S DRAWINGS OF SIRIUS SHOWS MULTIPLE STAR SYSTEMS. AT THE TIME THEY DREW THIS IMAGE, THE SECOND STAR SIRIUS B WAS UNDISCOVERED. MANY BELIEVE THERE IS ALSO A THIRD STAR, OR MORE, IN THE SIRIUS STAR SYSTEM, AS THIS DOGON DRAWING DEPICTS.

The star that the Dogon spoke of (long before scientists had verified its existence) is known as *Sirius B*. Once a main-sequence star, composed mostly of carbon, oxygen, hydrogen, and helium, Sirius B transitioned into a "red giant," before it finally "imploded" and became a "white dwarf" star.

Were the Nommos forced to leave their home planet because the star's transformation made it inhospitable, and did they come to Earth and create the bodies of water based on their knowledge of hydrogen and oxygen (the building blocks of water)?

THE AFRICAN DOGON TRIBE'S IMAGE OF THE NOMMOS, PRIMORDIAL BEINGS WHO VISITED THEM FROM SIRIUS B, CREATED BODIES OF WATER, AND TAUGHT THEM HOW TO FISH.

Located just above the northern border of the African continent, Syria is one of the most ancient civilizations on Earth, with populations of Sumerians, Babylonians, and Assyrians occupying territory that eventually spread from Mesopotamia to Turkey. It's where the first sighting of a mermaid was recorded, as well as the area where agriculture and cattle raising were introduced. Did the Nommos, amphibious beings with fish tails, visit Syria? Was Syria, consequently, named after Sirius?

Syria is the first place where mermaids were recorded in modern history. It's also very near to Africa, where creation stories speak of merpeople arriving on the planet to teach about agriculture and fishing for food.

Kiev
UKRAINE
Istanbul
Ankara
GREECE
TURKEY
SYRIA
IRAQ
IRAN
JORDAN
KUW
ANEAN SEA
CASPIAN SE
Cairo
BAHRAIN
Riyadh
LIBYA
EGYPT
Nile R.
SAUDI
ARABIA
RED SEA
Khartoum
ERITREA
CHAD

During the Roman era, Syria was one of the most populous and wealthiest provinces in the world. Did the Nommos from the star Sirius help them to boost their population and prosperity? Syria is also where the Apostle Paul underwent his conversion on the Road to Damascus, which led to his work helping establish the Christian church. Syria certainly is an extremely powerful region, which recently has been the site of great tension and warfare.

The Dogon say that the Nommos created bodies of water because they had to live in water to survive. Could this explain the great percentage of water on the earth's surface? After all, scientists can't explain how three-quarters of the earth came to be covered in water—a much greater percentage than on other planets. Scientists are also at a loss to explain how it has remained in liquid form for so many years, when other planets' considerably smaller water sources freeze or evaporate.

The Blue Star

From our earthly viewpoint, Sirius appears to be blue, with flickers of red and white. The ancients called its color "water blue." Even though Sirius is

over eight light-years away from Earth, it's one of our closest star neighbors. Its proximity makes Sirius the brightest star in the sky.

Whether it's an unconscious nod to our Sirius connection, or the product of governments' knowledge of the true connection we all have to this star system, red, white, and blue coloring is the theme of many of our world's flags. It's estimated that three-quarters of all nations have red in their flags, slightly fewer have white, and about half of all flags have blue in them.

Stars, too, are reflected in a high percentage of national flags. Approximately 67 flags feature them (out of 195 countries total in the world). I counted 36 flags from Africa with stars. Could this be because of Africa's close association with Sirius? The American flag depicts 50 stars, which is the number of rotations Sirius makes around the earth each year.

A six-pointed star (hexagram) is the symbol of both Judaism (the Star of David) and Vishnu, the Hindu creator god. Hermes Trismegistus, the founder of Hermeticism, hailed from Sirius, according to Egyptian legend. He was a teacher on Atlantis who moved to Egypt after the fabled continent was destroyed. His symbol is also a six-pointed star.

THE SIX-POINTED STAR IS THE SYMBOL OF JUDAISM; VISHNU, THE HINDU CREATOR DEITY; AND HERMES TRISMEGISTUS, THE ATLANTEAN TEACHER AND WRITER OF HERMETIC TEXTS.

The five-pointed star (or pentagram) is on the flags of 35 countries, including the United States, usually in "Sirian" colors of red, blue, or white. It is also the symbol of the nature-based spiritual path of Wicca. I believe the five-pointed star is symbolic of the human body, with the head, two arms, and two legs representing the five points.

What's more, law enforcement and military personnel normally also wear star insignias and badges to represent authority. And students receive a star on their homework when they've done a good job!

Many religions, such as Judaism and Hinduism, and cultures, including those of Egypt, Babylonia, and China, hold blue as a sacred color, as do sects such as the Masons and Druids. Blue is associated with value and valor. Perhaps that's where phrases such as *true blue, blue blood,* and *blue ribbon* originated.

Photo by Doreen Virtue

$\mathcal{S}$IRIUS A, B, AND C ARE DISPLAYED IN THIS CEILING MURAL AT THE HARRODS STORE IN LONDON.

22

Even the iconic store Harrods, in London, pays homage to Sirius in its ceiling mural of Isis (a mermaid) and Egyptian deities. This mural shows the three stars of Sirius—A, B, and C. In the lower right-hand corner, the dog in the mural has three five-pointed stars next to him, signifying the three stars of the Dog Star.

*T*HIS DOG IN THE HARRODS CEILING MURAL HAS THREE FIVE-POINTED STARS NEXT TO IT, REPRE-SENTING THE DOG STAR, WITH THREE STARS IN ITS SYSTEM: SIRIUS A, B, AND C.

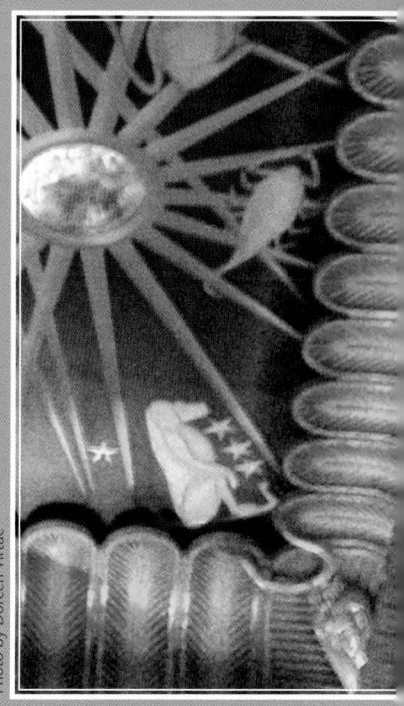

Photo by Doreen Virtue

AN OBJECT ON GOOGLE SKY BLOCKS US FROM SEEING SIRIUS, AND IS A CONTINUATION OF THE SECRETIVENESS OF THIS STAR SYSTEM'S POWERS.

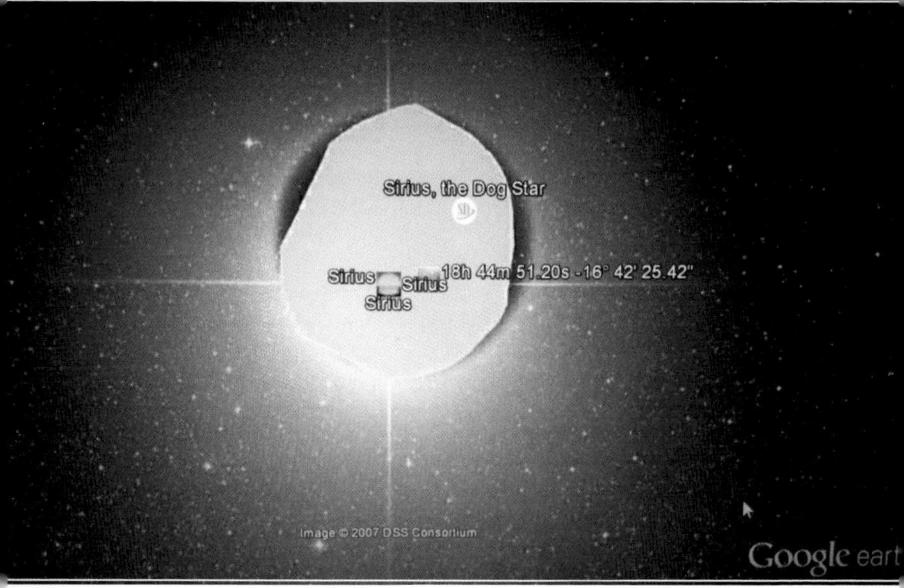

Sirius, the Dog Star

Sirius 18h 44m 51.20s -16° 42' 25.42"
Sirius Sirius
Sirius

Image © 2007 DSS Consortium

Google earth

Symbols and nods to Sirius are often secretive and accompanied by worldly success (such as Harrods), as if the energy of Sirius is being channeled as a source of manifestation energy. Is this knowledge guarded because it could be misused, or is the secretiveness from selfish intentions? Is this why the star system Sirius is blocked from view on Google Sky, the photographic map of the galaxy (as of the time of this book's printing in 2012)?

THE NAME STARBUCKS IMPLIES THAT THE STARS ARE BRINGING ABUNDANCE TO THE COMPANY FOUNDERS. THE LOGO HAS THREE STARS AS SYMBOLS.

Another abundantly successful company, Starbucks, has a logo with three five-pointed stars (one on the mermaid's crown and two on either side of the name. The name Starbucks, although said to be

25

taken from a Pacific Northwest coal mine ("Starbo"), implies that they're receiving money (*bucks* means "money" in American English slang) from the stars.

I've long researched the power of water to aid healing and manifestation. For instance, many people (myself included) gain insights and epiphanies while in the shower, bathtub, or near bodies of water. Studies show that the negative ions within nearby water sources increase the brain's alpha-wave amplitude, which leads to clear thinking and creative insights. My *Magical Mermaids and Dolphins Oracle Cards* may be used to give readings about manifestation because water represents the emotions and the unconscious mind's beliefs. So, spending time in or around water can help you find creative solutions and new ideas.

There's also a reason why healing wells are prevalent around the world. Water holds the charges of intentions and prayers, so it can transfer healing energy when it's applied topically to the skin or consumed as a beverage. It's best to say a blessing prior to drinking or applying any liquid, as it has a crystalline ability to respond to your intentions.

How fascinating that so many deities are depicted with blue bodies or auras, such as Shiva, Vishnu, Mother Mary, Archangel Michael, the Brazilian

water deity Yemanja, the Egyptian god Amun, and Krishna!

All of this veneration of blue and stars is a sign of respect to the star system Sirius. After all, the shafts within the pyramids of Egypt were constructed to point directly at Sirius during the height of its cycle, and to help humans predict when the Nile River would flood (in response to Sirius's cycles). There is a great deal of evidence that the construction of Washington, D.C., was also oriented around Sirius. The Washington Monument recalls Egyptian hiero-glyphic representations of Sirius as an obelisk.

Sirius, the Mother Star

Sirius is believed to be the inspiration for the Star of David and the star of Bethlehem (the Christmas star). One of the brightest stars, it is often referred to as the "God Star" or the "Dog Star." Sirius is 25 times more luminous than our sun, and twice as big. It is also twice as bright as the next-brightest star, Cano-pus. Scientists say that Earth is "downstream" from the starlight of Sirius, which means that the star sys-tem is continuously sending us light.

Sirius is actually composed of two stars, dubbed Sirius A and Sirius B, which are 8.6 light-years from Earth (that's relatively close). Many believe there is a third star within the Sirius system (and perhaps more). Sirius B was only discovered relatively recently, even though the Dogon tribe discussed and drew the second star for years prior.

After the sun, Sirius is the closest star visible to the bare human eye from most of Earth. Hundreds of millions of years ago, both Sirius A and B were main-sequence stars, until the latter became a red giant and then collapsed into its current state as a white dwarf.

Since ancient times, Sirius has been worshipped and depicted in carvings and artwork. When the star rises in June, the Nile River also rises and provides life-sustaining water for crops. Ancient people believed that Sirius provided spiritual light, while the sun provided physical light. They also believed that great spiritual teachers (and gods and goddesses) originated from Sirius. This was especially true among the Egyptians, whose pantheon members, such as Isis, Horus, Osiris, and others, were associated with Sirius. The Greeks, Sumerians, and Babylonians also held that their deities came from this star.

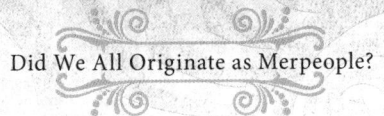

Today, Sirius is still revered, including figuring prominently in Freemasonry symbols (referred to as the "Blazing Star," it is the source of divine power, and the place where divine souls will return to). Many believe that the capstone of the Great Pyramid (which is aligned with Sirius) on the back of the U.S. dollar bill depicts the light of Sirius. This shows the Sirian connection to supply and abundance. Even the organization within the Masons that is open to females, called the Order of the Eastern Star, is based upon Sirius (the star of the east). Sirius is also represented by the Star card among Tarot's major arcana.

Mother Mary is frequently called *Stella Maris,* or the "Star of the Sea." In paintings, the star depicted with her is Sirius.

MOTHER MARY IS FREQUENTLY CALLED THE "STAR OF THE SEA," AS PORTRAYED IN THIS IMAGE OF HER WITH THE STAR SIRIUS.

The constellation Cassiopeia forms a large inverted letter *M* in the northern hemisphere, which is believed to stand for "Mother" or "Mer," as in the sea and the water-born mermaids and mermen. As mentioned earlier, the words for ocean and mother are related in many languages. *Mara* means "of the sea" in Gaelic, and many girls are named Mary in honor of the Blessed Mother (Star of the Sea).

Mermaids and the Mayan Culture

When I visited a Mayan shaman and historian named Manuel Zaldivar at Chichén Itzá, site of the ruins of an ancient city in Mexico, he told me that Mayan culture originated with the Olmecs, who migrated from Africa to Mexico. He said, "The Olmecs were the mother Mesoamerican culture, and the first to build pyramids in southern Mexico and South America."

Manuel told me: "Much of the story of Creation is written in our sacred Mayan book, *Popol Vuh*. Mayans believe that in the beginning was darkness, and life came out of the sea, and then light followed. Life came from four Creator Mothers from the water who married gods. The first Creator Mother was

Caha-Pahma, whose name means 'standing water falling from above.' The Creator Mothers who followed were Chomiha, meaning 'beautiful chosen water'; Tzununiha, which translates into 'water of hummingbirds'; and Caquixaha, meaning 'water of the macaw.'

"Mayans believe that all life came from the ocean. Water is used in sacred rituals. In fact, the name Itzá (as in Chichén Itzá) means 'the well of the water sorcerers.'"

Manuel explained that these sorcerers worked with water elementals such as sprites and undines, who carried out the sorcerers' requests. He said that humans once knew how to levitate and possessed the ability to perform other miraculous feats, "but we lost it because we began eating meat and getting intoxicated. Once you lose your god-abilities, it's difficult to get them back. This is not so much a punishment, as it is a result of lowering your energy with meat and alcohol."

CHAPTER THREE

THE MERPEOPLE REALM

As I swam under the lapis-hued ocean waters of Bora-Bora several years ago, I received a "download" of information. I've always had this experience of water opening me up to hearing detailed and profound information. Sometimes this occurs in the shower or bathtub, or while I'm sitting next to a lake or other body of water. More commonly, though, I find that being actually under saltwater (either free diving, scuba diving, or snorkeling) opens me up to

the divine. My guidance has told me that negative energy cannot permeate the surface of saltwater, which is a purifying and protecting agent that can detoxify you, whether you drink it or bathe in it. You can even detoxify your sinuses by using a saltwater inhaler such as a neti pot.

The message I received had to do with people's different eye colors, as they relate to each individual's element. For example, I was told that people with brown eyes had strong connections with the earth and its spirituality, such as animals, birds, trees, crystals, plants, and fairies. Those with blue eyes were associated with the air element and were attuned to angels and extraterrestrials. People with yellow-tinged brown eyes were connected to the fire element and beings of fire, such as Archangel Michael and the goddesses Brigit and Pele. Those with green eyes were associated with water, and so could easily connect with fish, marine mammals, seabirds, and mermaids.

This information surprised me, even as it intuitively resonated as the truth. I'd written the books *Earth Angels* and *Realms of the Earth Angels,* about the various realms that lightworkers originated from, based upon similar messages I'd received. Those who read these books usually report that doing so helps

THE TRANQUILITY OF THE SEA AND THE MERMAID.

them understand themselves better. They tell me that it's a relief to know the reasons for their habits, relationship patterns, and likes and dislikes.

Ever since I'd written about these realms (which include Incarnated Angels, Incarnated Elementals, Wise Ones, Merpeople, and Starpeople), I continued to receive more information about new ones and hybrid blends of realms. At each of my Angel Therapy Practitioner® and Angel Intuitive™ courses, I'd ask my students to gather together and assemble a meeting with people of their Earth Angel realm. There, we were able to really see and study the similarities among each realm's members.

I'd noticed that Merpeople of all races share some characteristics:

- ☆ They have auburn-red tones in their blond, brunette, or black hair.

- ☆ They all have some shade of green in their eyes, either as pure green, hazel brown with green, or blue with green.

I decided to create a survey to discover whether these patterns held true in larger samples. I placed a notice in my monthly newsletter, asking those who resonated with the definition of Merpeople to please

complete my survey. I asked participants to identify whether they thought they were definitely a Merperson, probably a Merperson, or undecided.

I selected only the surveys of those who said they were definitely a Merperson. Most based this opinion on the fact that they matched my descriptions—for example, they *had* to live near water to feel emotionally balanced, they'd identified with mermaids or mermen since childhood, they had frequent dreams about mermaids, and so on.

Of all the findings of the survey, the significant ones were:

- 82 percent of respondents had a natural red tint or red highlights in their hair.

- 82 percent preferred to wear their hair long (including 89 percent of the females surveyed).

- 79 percent had naturally curly or wavy hair.

- 69 percent had green in their eyes.

- 85 percent reported being frequently or constantly thirsty for water.

⋆ 80 percent said they felt cold often,
   even in warm weather.

The 82 percent of red- and auburn-haired re-spondents eclipses the estimated 2 to 10 percent of people with naturally red or auburn hair in the general population. Apparently, red hair is a genetic anomaly.

At one time, red-haired women were the tar-gets of witchcraft accusations. In the 16th and 17th centuries, redheaded European women were put to death during the witch-hunting crusades. Could they have been Merpeople who retained their magi-cal abilities and knowledge? Were they water sorcer-esses, such as I'd learned about in the Mayan culture, who were granted favors from the water Elementals or undines?

Many of the mer-survey participants described their measures to stay healthy and warm, including taking frequent sea-salt baths, eating kelp or sea-weed-based foods, taking frequent vacations in warm tropical locales, and avoiding cold-weather climates.

THOSE FROM THE MER REALM
ARE IRRESISTIBLY DRAWN
TO THE OCEAN.

One woman told me, "Since I was three years old, I knew how to swim without any lessons. I have to wrap my feet in wet towels every night to avoid pain. I also have scales on my legs that no cream or dermatologist has been able to cure. I move in the water like a mermaid, and once set a world record for my butterfly stroke, even though I've never received any formal training."

According to Mark Eddowes, an archaeologist and historian of Polynesia and the author of *Moorea of the Society Islands,* the earliest settlers in Tahiti and surrounding islands were the Tamahu people. They had white skin, reddish-blond hair, and green-hazel eyes. The Tamahu preceded the European settlers, and they were considered to be beings of great beauty. Their hair was said to hold sacred *mana* (energy), and was often fashioned into sacred ornaments.

Mark's research about a red-haired, green-eyed population who suddenly appeared made me think of Atlantis's Merperson connection. As Atlantis was sinking, some people escaped by shape-shifting into dolphins, others swam away as mermaids or mermen, and still others rode atop dolphins to safety. They all made their way to Africa, South America, Greece, Italy, Mexico, Australia, or Polynesia, where their Atlantean knowledge of pyramid building,

healing, and such formed the basis for the Egyptian, Mayan, Aztec, and other advanced cultures. Ancient legend says that Apollo was in dolphin form when he arrived in Greece (other legends say he rode a chariot pulled by dolphins, or rode atop them). A shrine called Delphi was built in Apollo's honor (*Delphi* means "dolphin love" in Greek). Many other deities, including Athena, Thoth, Metatron, Michael, and Merlin, were Atlantean leaders.

The Tahitians also believed in Merpeople, Mark told me. "*Meherio* is the Tahitian version of Merpeople, who are often seen as mermaids. They are positive beings who protect those lost at sea. Often they morph into beautiful girls who come onto the land at sunset to seduce young warriors and chiefs. The Meherio talk these men into returning with them in the morning, in secret, back to the sea. The Meherio generally give birth to exceptional beings in the human world, but nearly always after being briefly with the humans, they return to the sea."

Does this legend remind you of Hans Christian Andersen's "The Little Mermaid"? Andersen's story is based upon the archetypal tale of a mermaid seducing and marrying a mortal.

Mark also told me about the Tahitian deity Tinirau, who's half man and half shark. He watches

over people who are half shark as well. The Tahitians believe humans originated from the ocean, and we share a common ancestry with the dolphins, sharks, and other sea creatures.

I asked Rose Rosetree, who has studied face and energy reading since 1975 and is the author of *The Power of Face Reading,* if she'd noticed any distinguishing characteristics correlated with people's eye colors. I didn't tell her about my own research to avoid influencing her answer.

Rose told me that she'd definitely noticed strong personality traits associated with eye colors:

* Blue-eyed people were more geared toward ideas and intellectualism. This fit with the element of air, which is associated with the intellect.

* Green-eyed people were more emotional, especially if they also had red hair. This fit with the element of water, which is related to emotions.

* Brown-eyed people were down-to-earth, which fit in with the earth element.

☆ People with yellow in their brown eyes were intensely passionate, which fit in with the fire element.

In meditation, I once heard:

All human bodies are mer-bodies, built for the water. Everyone is a Merperson of one form or another. The green-eyed, auburn-haired people seem to have the most mer-characteristics because they were the last to come out of the water and live upon land. In the meantime, the others were exploring other realms of the vast universe, or upon the great planet Earth.

So those with green in their eyes and red in their hair are like the children who stay in the swimming pool until closing time!

Hybrids of the Merperson Realm

There are hybrids or combinations of several Earth Angel realms that are connected to Merpeople (for more information, please read my book *Realms of the Earth Angels*).

Merpeople must live near bodies of water to feel happy and healthy. Merfairies are drawn to rivers and lakes, while Merangels, Mystic Mers, and Star-Mers feel connected to the ocean. Many Merpeople have memories of, or are attracted to, stories about Atlantis and Lemuria (another ancient oceanic civilization).

As with other realms, Merpeople look like their spiritual counterparts. Female Merpeople resemble mermaids, with curvy, hourglass figures and a penchant for wearing turquoise-colored clothing. Mermen look athletic, trim, and outdoorsy. Both genders prefer wearing their hair long, and their tresses have natural waves. The majority have a naturally red tint in their hair.

Merpeople report feeling cold easily, and they prefer to vacation or live in tropical climates. As much as they love the water, though, Merpeople avoid swimming pools because they're sensitive to the smell and feel of chlorine.

Merpeople are frequently thirsty, and many have issues with constipation. They usually have a bottle of water at hand, and they do best avoiding dried fruit, which tends to deplete their systems of fluids. Their water sensitivity also causes Merpeople to be very choosy about which brand of bottled water

they drink. Merpeople often crave seaweed salad, sea vegetables, and nori (flattened seaweed, wrapped around sushi rolls), probably because their bodies need the special sea-based nutrients.

Most people love dolphins, but Merpeople are fanatical about them. Merpeople also love whales, seabirds, seahorses, and other water-dwelling beings. Many Merpeople volunteer time or money to support charities or events that protect the oceans, lakes, and rivers. Their favorite vacation destination is a tropical beach, and they either live near a body of water or long to do so. Merpeople also diligently pick up litter from beaches and lakefronts.

There are several Merpeople subcategories, including:

— **Merangels.** As a hybrid of half Incarnated Angel (an angel who assumes human form) and half Elemental (mermaids are part of the Elemental realm), Merangels vacillate between being naughty and nice. Female Merangels may resemble Incarnated Angels, with their voluptuous bodies; heart-shaped, youthful faces; and tumbling, highlighted hair. Yet they are the Incarnated Angels who've lived on the edge. They may have histories of drug and alcohol abuse, relationship betrayals, and even

criminal records. However, their hearts are purely angelic at the core.

— **Merfairies.** This hybrid is 100 percent Elemental, so Merfairies have no apologies about being "party animals" at the ocean, lakes, or rivers. They enjoy cocktails while watching seaside sunsets, boating, or lazing on a beach. Merfairies tend to be perfectionistic about their romantic partners, which may lead to a long succession of boyfriends and girlfriends. Yet Merfairies will tell you that they're trying to find lifelong satisfaction, in the form of a fun, financially secure—oh, and did I mention *fun?*—relationship. Merfairies love to camp, hike, and be next to lakes and rivers set in the mountains. They have a special bond with the water fairies (sprites and undines).

— **Star-Mers.** Most Starpeople (those with ties to extraterrestrials and the celestial realm) love being near the ocean, but this hybrid is especially drawn to the sea. Star-Mers are loners who prefer to sail, swim, surf, or snorkel by themselves (or with one special and trusted companion). Star-Mers particularly love to look at the starry skies while drifting on a boat in the middle of the ocean. They connect with their home planets through the energy of the water's positive ions.

— **Mercherubs.** Similar to Merangels, except that the "angel half" is from the cherub realm, Mercherubs are usually petite with very cute, childlike faces. They are extremely romantic and fall in love easily. They have expensive tastes and adore luxury spas, designer clothes, and five-star travel. They like to live near the ocean, but much prefer looking at the sea to swimming in it, because they don't want to muss their hair with saltwater or sand.

— **Mystic Mers.** This hybrid realm is a blend of Merperson and Wise One (a reincarnated sorcerer or sorceress, high priestess, wizard, shaman, or witch). They have the edgy Elemental personality combined with the seriousness of Wise Ones. They love to teach, especially about dolphins, whales, Atlantis, ocean ecology, scuba diving, sailing, or any other

48

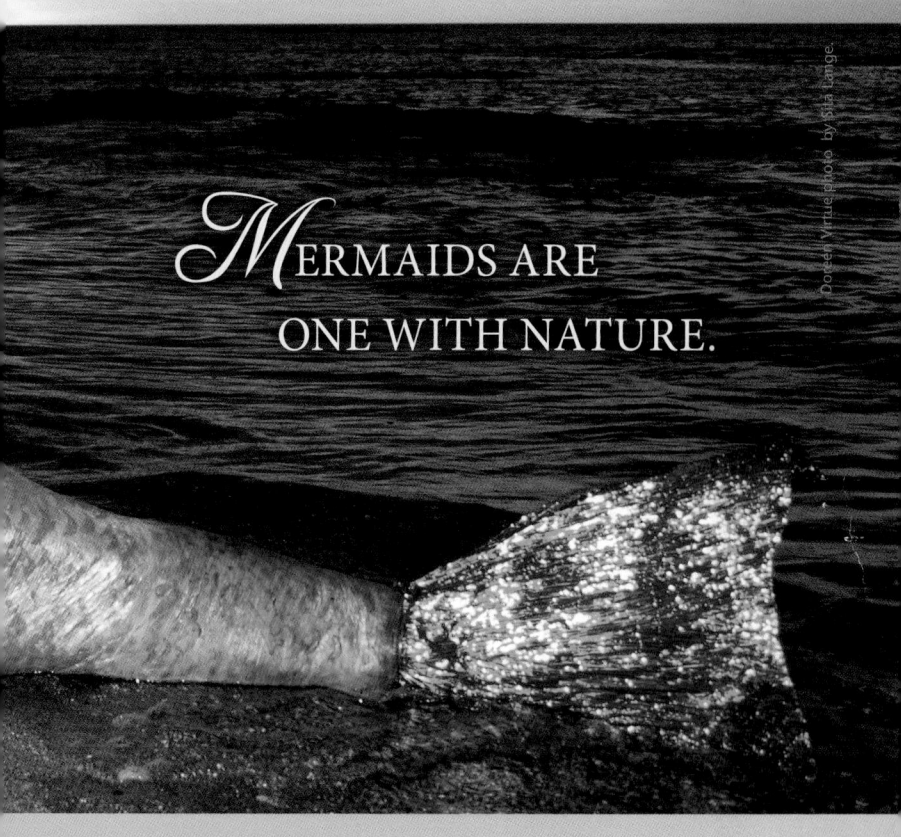

MERMAIDS ARE ONE WITH NATURE.

area related to the ocean. A subcategory of this realm is Mystic Merangels, who are a blend of an Incarnated Angel, Merperson, and Wise One.

— **Atlanteans.** Those who lived during the time of Atlantis are hybrids of Incarnated Angels, Wise Ones, and Merpeople. They are fascinated with Egyptian spirituality and symbols, including

pyramids. They usually have dark hair and stand and walk with perfect posture. While they love the ocean, most have phobias of swimming because of their sudden drowning deaths when Atlantis fell.

In the next chapter, we'll examine another mer category called "Incarnated Dolphins."

🐚 🐚 🐚

CHAPTER FOUR

INCARNATED DOLPHINS

Incarnated Dolphins are a hybrid of the Merpeople realm, and consist of dolphins who have taken on human form so that their message is clearly heard by people. Yet their appearance betrays their true identity. Incarnated Dolphins' bodies are shaped like *actual* dolphin bodies. A slightly protruding belly casts their silhouette with the same dimensions as an American football. Most Incarnated Dolphins have gray eyes.

Incarnated Dolphins also express amusement with the same snickering laugh as ocean-dwelling

DOLPHINS LOVE SWIMMING AND PLAYING WITH MERMAIDS.

dolphins. Most have sea-related professions such as oceanographer, boat captain, or ocean ecologist. They're passionate about preserving the marine ecology and make wonderful teachers in this area. Yet, because of their dolphin origin, they know how to relax, play, and flirt while meeting their responsibilities. Because they're accustomed to swimming in pods, Incarnated Dolphins are usually very social. They love long and lighthearted discussions. They're laid-back people who prefer to sleep and socialize, rather than work hard.

For example, a woman I know named Gayle loves dolphins, and regularly leads group excursions to swim with them in exotic locations. She even looks like a dolphin, with her sleekly rounded body and oval eyes. Interestingly, Gayle runs a swimming-pool company. Her sun sign is Pisces—the fish—a water sign.

She says, "I love the ocean and *have* to spend time there to recharge. I love dolphins and whales, and spend much time in the ocean swimming with them. I asked my guides why I feel so connected to the ocean, and I was told, 'Because, Gayle, you are *of* the ocean.' At first, I didn't understand what that meant. Now I do believe that I may have been a dolphin before."

In addition to Incarnated Dolphins, I've also met a few Incarnated Whales—and, no, they're not obese. While Incarnated Dolphins have a playful, Elemental personality, Incarnated Whales have the protective and loving energy of archangels. Both Incarnated Dolphins and Whales often become advocates, activists, marine biologists, sailors, or scuba divers.

An Angel Therapist and friend of mine named Lisa Weiss—who sports long, flowing red hair; green eyes; and a genuine smile—told me that her interest in mermaids started when she worked with marine animals during her college days.

"I had recurring dreams about people being able to swim underwater without coming up for air," she said. "Then I had a lucid dream that I was digging in the dirt and found a shroud that reminded me of the Shroud of Turin, except the image was of a dolphin glowing with a neon-blue outline. I heard a high-pitched tone emitted from the dolphin image, followed by thousands of nondescript voices that seemed to be downloading information to me.

"Then the dolphin in the shroud came alive and it told me, 'We lived on land at one time. We were

one with the humans.' The dolphin told me that his species was once humanlike when they'd walked on the earth. They shape-shifted and moved into the ocean after humans began misusing their power and abusing the environment. The dolphins believed that if they got away from humans and lived on their own in the ocean, they could wait until that time when humans became more peaceful and environmentally conscious. Then the dolphin looked at me and clearly said, 'Now it's time, so we're coming back to take over the world.'"

That was in 1988, a time when Lisa hadn't read any New Age books, had no knowledge of Atlantis, and had a very "left-brained" understanding of dolphins. So the dream frightened her, which led her to do metaphysical research. "Now I have a very positive outlook on the dream's meaning," Lisa explained, "and since that time, I've received so many signs that point to the return of the dolphins."

She tapped her left cheek and said, "This is one of the signs." There, etched on Lisa's skin, was a perfect purple image of a jumping dolphin. It wasn't a birthmark or tattoo—this was like a "wine stain" in a very precise shape. "It appeared on my face immediately following my dolphin dream," she explained.

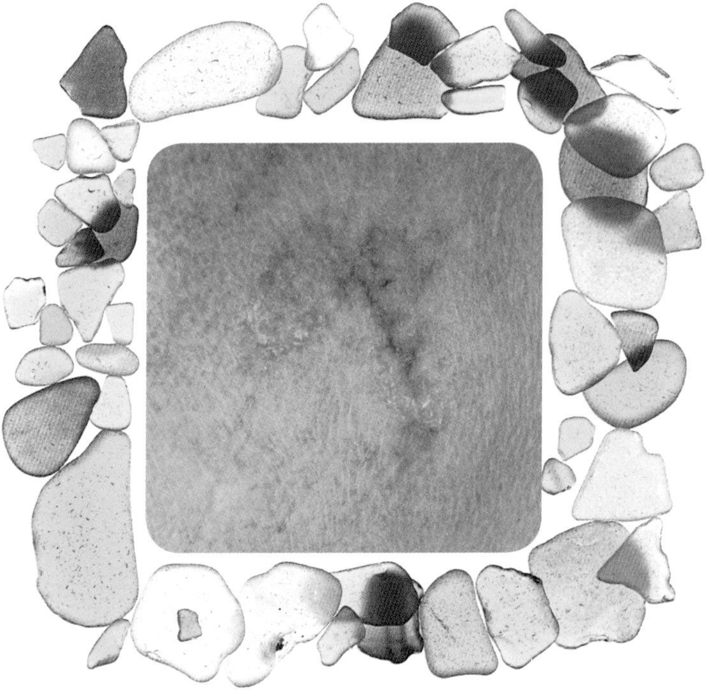

$\mathcal{T}$HIS JUMPING DOLPHIN SUDDENLY
APPEARED ON LISA WEISS'S LEFT CHEEK
IN 1988 AND HAS NOT FADED SINCE.

As part of her research, Lisa had a past-life regression. "When the hypnotherapist took me through a gate into my past life, I fell into water. The hypnotherapist asked me to look down at my feet and describe the type of shoes I was wearing. Well, I didn't have feet—I had dolphin fins!" Lisa tried two more regressions, with the same results.

Another time, a psychic who knew nothing of Lisa's dream or past-life reading told her, "You were a dolphin in your past life."

Messages from Dolphins

I've been fortunate enough to spend a lot of hours in the ocean with wild dolphins. Sometimes I'll do this while swimming or snorkeling, with the dolphins on either side of me. I've also been deep underwater scuba diving, gliding belly-to-belly with them. On a few occasions, I was riding upon an underwater scooter while scuba diving and was able to do spins and flips with the dolphins.

When I put on my mermaid tail and swim with dolphins, I feel even closer to them. Since dolphins are about the same size as humans, it's easy to imagine our physiological connection.

When swimming with dolphins, I see geometric energy like neon-colored scaffolding around them, forming the shapes of triangles. These energy triangles surround each dolphin and travel with them as they swim. Most of the energy triangles are electric blue.

Are these triangular energy shapes around the dolphins part of the energy complex of their sonar system? Were the pyramids erected in Atlantis, Egypt, and Mayan and other civilizations in honor of these powerful shapes? Or are the triangles and pyramids connector portals to our Creator or star system? The cobalt-blue color certainly is reflective of Sirius.

In a meditation I had with the Archangel Raziel (whose name means "the Secrets of God" in Hebrew), I asked him about the connection between dolphins, mermaids, and humans.

He replied immediately:

> *They're simultaneous beings who coexist in different dimensions, depending upon where your focus is directed. If you only focus upon dolphins, that's all you'll see, but if you look holographically at the energy of dolphins, you'll see their energy grids, as well as the humans*

THE DOLPHINS LOVE TO SWIM WITH MERMAIDS, AS THIS PHOTO OF ME SWIMMING IN MY MERMAID TAIL IN KONA, HAWAII, SHOWS.

Doreen Virtue photo © Susan Knight Studios.

merged with dolphins, who are the Merpeople, and the dolphins merged with angels, who are the Merangels.

The rainbow spectrum will increase the human brain's serotonin levels, in the same way that the rainbow rays within natural sunlight act as antidepressants. You were given rainbows within light to free and illuminate your inner rainbow of chakras. That's why you need sunshine to stay bright and healthy.

He explained that the dolphins bring the rainbow ray of light to us, which is one of the aspects of their healing ability. He said:

Water has memory and holds energy. That's why the water at Lourdes, Brigit's Well, Chalice Well, and other healing wells has powerful effects. The water is imbued with the loving energy of goddesses and angels, as well as with prayers offered by people asking for healing. Water is rainbow droplets that heal in the same way crystal prisms refract light into rainbow spectrums.

Our Dolphin Ancestors

Dolphins first appeared on Earth between 23.8 million and 16.4 million years ago, while modern humans didn't make an appearance until 200,000 years ago. So we are relative newcomers to our 4.5-billion-year-old planet.

Researchers at Texas A&M University discovered that humans and dolphins have a similar genome and share many of the same genes. Sadly, increasing numbers of dolphins have been dying off, populations are experiencing reductions in reproductive output, and extremely high toxicity levels have been found in studied animals. The researchers concluded that environmental pollution could be similarly affecting humans.

Lisa Weiss continues to connect to the dolphins, and helps other people to do the same. She says, "The most important lesson the dolphins emphasize is that every living thing really is connected. Every action, thought, emotion, and word ignites a chain reaction that ripples through the organism of life! Our awareness of that Oneness is the key to all other lessons. When we know this, with all that we are, we will be more likely to make a conscious effort to send out ripples that cause peace, happiness, harmony, love, and health. When we hurt one, we hurt all. When we love one, we love all!"

Like me and others who are tuned in to the energy of the environment, Lisa has received a message with a wake-up call about Mother Earth. I am concerned that dolphins may be going the way of unicorns, unless we decontaminate the ocean and stop using disruptively loud underwater sonar. Many of us hear the cry to quickly replace fossil fuels with sustainable solar and wind power. The dolphins ask us to speak up and take action on behalf of the environment, such as only eating sustainable fish (avoiding bluefin tuna and Chilean sea bass, for example) or by abstaining from fish altogether. We also must clean up the Great Pacific Garbage Patch—plastic debris caught in a gyre (a giant circular oceanic surface current)—and take care not to dump further chemicals and plastics in the ocean. By switching to eco-friendly laundry detergent and shampoos, and demanding that disruptively loud underwater military sonar be reduced, we can make a huge contribution toward ocean health.

Dolphins are our family members, with connections to Atlantis, as we'll look at in the next chapter.

CHAPTER FIVE

ATLANTIS

I took an advanced class of Angel Therapy Prac-
titioners through an Atlantean past-life regression:

*Let's begin by getting comfortable in your
chair, or even lying down if you prefer. Please
take some deep breaths, inhaling deeply and
then exhaling completely.*

*Now allow yourself to see a dolphin. This
is your personal dolphin guide, who will take
you on your journey back to your life in Atlantis.
When you feel ready, please climb onto the dolphin for this journey.*

*A big, bright rainbow has just appeared in
front of you. Please choose one of the colors of*

the rainbow rays, as a pathway for you and your dolphin to travel upon. You and your dolphin are now gliding up the rainbow toward the top of the arc.

As you glide downward toward the vast blue ocean, you're entering the time of Atlantis. You are now in Atlantis. Please look at your feet and notice whether they've changed in any way. Notice your surroundings and who's around you. Notice where you are and what's going on.

If you haven't already done so, please transport yourself to a Healing Temple. Notice the details of the temple: Who's in there with you? What are they doing? What are <u>you</u> doing? Spend as much time in this temple as you'd like.

When you're ready, please go to a place in Atlantis that was significant for you during your lifetime there. What do you see? Who's with you? Do you notice any crystals around you?

When you feel ready, please return with your dolphin to the rainbow. Choose a color to ride upon as you slowly and gently return to your present life. You can bring all your knowledge from Atlantis along with you, and you can return to Atlantis anytime you like. Your dolphin will stay with you to assist, heal, and love you.

As the class returned their awareness to the present day, many were in tears, sobbing because they missed the great love they'd felt in Atlantis.

After we'd processed the grief of leaving the "lost continent," I next connected with the energy of Hermes, the great Atlantean high priest and spiritual leader. Hermes left Atlantis before its downfall and went to Egypt, where he was known as Thoth or Hermes Trismegistus (meaning "three times great"), and to England, where he was called Merlin.

Hermes said that his name was a play on words: "My name is actually: *He's Mer.*" Hermes had a mer-connection to Atlantis, and transported himself away from the flooded continent with his mer-abilities. This ability to transport himself gave him the Roman name Mercury, which also has the prefix *Mer-* in it. Hermes also took on the persona of Merlin the magician, again with his signature "Mer" in his name.

I asked the class to write about their memories of Atlantis. I compiled their answers with a survey I'd taken of people who listened to the guided meditation of the Atlantean Healing Temples on my CD *Angel Medicine,* as well as audience members who had also participated in a similar Atlantean regression.

One woman reported about her Atlantean experience: "As I looked around this amazing place, I felt real peace. Every cell of my being was at one with each other, at one with all. I felt so relaxed, secure, and alive—truly alive—like never before. I felt that I was home!"

All of the surveys and writings about Atlantean experiences described similar scenarios:

- ⭐ People were dressed in long white robes, gowns, or tunics with golden ropes as belts.

- ⭐ Men and women wore their hair long, and it was dark in color.

- ⭐ People had very large feet with webbed toes. Sometimes their feet were finned, especially when the person was swimming in the ocean (their feet were changeable).

- ⭐ People could breathe while swimming underwater by pulling oxygen out of the water in their mouths, which functioned much like fish gills.

- ⭐ Dolphins coexisted alongside people.

⭐ Some people reported that they shape-shifted into mermaids, mermen, or dolphins whenever they entered the water.

⭐ Pools and waterways ran through towns and often within healing temples. There were underground water tunnels that people and dolphins used to transport themselves.

⭐ Buildings were made of marble and crystal, with columns and pillars in most interiors. Some structures were round, and others were pyramid shaped.

⭐ There was a Shangri-la atmosphere, with waterfalls and beautiful trees and flowers.

The societies on Lemuria, another "lost land," and Atlantis were *antediluvian,* which means "before the great deluge described in Genesis and the pre-Judaic texts." Many cultures have legends about a great flood. The Babylonians' story is almost identical

to that of Noah and the ark, even including the release of a raven and a dove to check if the waters had subsided. Scientific evidence shows that a major comet hit the Mediterranean Sea around 3150 B.C., the time of Noah's flood. A previous comet impact in 7640 B.C. may have also besieged the earth. Lemuria is believed to have sunk in the earliest flood, and Atlantis in the second deluge.

In the next chapter, we'll look at our evolutionary connection to dolphins and other water-dwelling mammals, showing how all of us are Merpeople genetically.

CHAPTER SIX

THE AQUATIC APE

One night I had a dream about dolphins. Actually, it seemed more like a dolphin visitation than a dream. I woke up knowing that humans were biologically connected to dolphins, and I felt compelled to research this connection.

The dolphins themselves seemed to guide my research to a topic I'd never before heard of called the *aquatic ape hypothesis*. This theory states that the human body has many similarities to aquatic mammals such as dolphins, seals, and manatees. The aquatic ape hypothesis was first introduced by

Sir Alister Hardy, a Linacre Professor of Zoology at the University of Oxford, and then later popularized by Elaine Morgan, a British researcher and the author of *The Descent of Woman* (a play on the title of Charles Darwin's book on primate evolution, *The Descent of Man*).

According to the aquatic ape hypothesis, the human body evolved as our ancestors spent five to six hours daily swimming or wading in the water, finding and eating food such as sea vegetables. Hardy and Morgan point out the features that make the human body ideally suited for water environments:

— **Hairlessness.** Humans have "hairless" bodies, like other water mammals, so we can swim more efficiently. What hair we do have on our bodies grows in the same direction to facilitate swimming forward through water currents. Primates and other land-dwelling creatures have fur to protect them from the sun and other elements.

— **Subcutaneous fat.** Humans and water mammals have a substantial layer of subcutaneous (immediately under the skin) fat, which provides perfect insulation in cold waters.

— **Protruding female breasts.** Human female breasts are similar to those of female manatees. Protruding breasts are ideal for feeding babies while in the water, providing a way for babies to grasp on to the mother while nursing, and possibly helping with buoyancy and warmth. Female primates' breasts typically don't protrude.

— **Weeping.** Only water-dwelling mammals and humans weep tears when they're upset. Scientists believe the tear glands in water dwellers help balance the salt levels in the body, as well as eliminate waste products secreted during emotional stress. Primates and other land dwellers only secrete tears to moisturize the eyes or when they're ill, not to express emotions.

— **Nose flaps.** Human nostril muscles are similar to those of seals, in that we can partially close them to keep out water while swimming.

— **Hair on the head.** The reason why humans still have hair on their heads may lie within clues from indigenous cultures. Female members of an aboriginal tribe in Patagonia spend a lot of time in the water. If the women carried their babies in their arms while swimming, wading, or fishing, they'd

be thrown off balance. Instead, babies hold on to their mothers' long hair. Elaine Morgan contends that this may be why hair tends to grow thicker during pregnancy, and why women rarely go bald. This could also explain why 89 percent of the female Merpeople I surveyed prefer to wear their hair long. Perhaps this is also why mermaids in paintings are usually portrayed with long hair.

— **Webbing.** Humans have webbing between the thumb and index finger, unlike primates. We also have a small amount of webbing between our fingers, and a very small percentage of people are born with webbed toes.

— **Swimming.** Primates and land mammals swim with their heads above water. Only humans and water mammals dive and swim underwater.

— **Copulation.** Only water-dwelling mammals (and the bonobo, a rare species of ape) mate face-to-face. Human and aquatic-mammal genitals are located on the front of the body. Land-dwelling animals copulate with the male behind the female, mainly because mating in trees or on the open ground makes this the most stable position. The vagina of

most primates and land dwellers is situated beneath the tail.

— **Oil.** The millions of sebaceous glands on the face and scalp weren't designed to cause teenage angst over acne! The chief purpose of body-secreted oil is to provide waterproofing.

— **Breathing.** Humans and dolphins can control their breathing rate, a feat that allows them to purposely hold their breath before diving. The breathing rate of land dwellers, including primates, is automatically controlled, only changing as a reaction and not as a conscious plan. In addition, only humans, sea lions, and dugongs (a water mammal similar to a manatee) have a descended larynx, which keeps water out of the lungs while diving.

Hardy and Morgan argue that humans' diet chiefly consisted of fish and sea vegetables, which they obtained by diving or wading. This healthful "smart food" diet helped the human brain grow significantly larger proportionally than those of primates and land dwellers. Hardy believes that humans first developed tools to catch fish more efficiently, and because females gathered sea vegetables and fish while wading in cool waters, they developed more

subcutaneous fat in their lower bodies. (This theory certainly explains why female Merpeople and paintings of mermaids feature hourglass figures.)

The researchers also contend that the humans' upright posture is ideal for wading and swimming. One reason why so many people complain of back pain is that the human body is not built for living on land. In fact, the moment we stand up, our bodies react to the stress by immediately hoarding our inner salt supply.

Elaine Morgan writes:

> It is now generally agreed the man/ape split occurred in Africa between 7 and 5 million years ago, during a period known as the fossil gap. Before it, there was an animal which was the common ancestor of human and African apes. After it, there emerged a creature smaller than ourselves, but bearing the unmistakable hallmark of the first shift towards human status: it walked on two legs.
>
> This poses two questions: "Where were the earliest fossils found?" and "Do we know of anything happening in that place at that time that might have caused apes and humans to evolve along separate lines?" The oldest pre-human fossils (including the best known one, "Lucy") are

called *Australopithecus afarensis* because their bones were discovered in the afar triangle, an area of low lying land near the Red Sea. About 7 million years ago, that area was flooded by the sea and became the Sea of Afar.

Part of the ape population living there at the time would have found themselves living in a radically changed habitat. Some may have been marooned on off-shore islands—the present day Danakil Alps were once surrounded by water. Others may have lived in flooded forests, salt marshes, mangrove swamps, lagoons, or on the shores of the new sea, and they would all have had to adapt or die.

Aquatic Ape Theory suggests that some of them survived, and began to adapt to their watery environment. Much later, when the Sea of Afar became landlocked and finally evaporated, their descendants returned to the mainland of Africa and began to migrate southwards, following the waterways of the Rift Valley upstream.

There is nothing in the fossil record to invalidate this scenario, and much to sustain it. Lucy's bones were found at Afar lying among crocodile and turtle eggs and crab claws at the edge of a flood plain near what would have then been the coast of Africa.

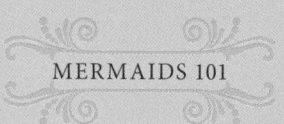

Other fossils of Australopithecus, dated later, were found further south, almost invariably in the immediate vicinity of ancient lakes and rivers. We now know that the change from the ape into Australopithecus took place in a short space of time, by evolutionary standards. Such rapid speciation is almost invariably a sign that one population of a species has become isolated by a geographical barrier such as a stretch of water.

Some of us are so connected to the ocean that we instinctively feel like we are mermaids and mermen. We even wear mermaid and mermen tails and swim in the sea, lakes, and pools, as you'll read and see in the next chapter.

CHAPTER SEVEN

SWIMMING WITH A MERMAID TAIL

Ever since the movie *Splash* came out in 1984, there's been a call for "swimmable" mermaid tails. Until recently, though, such tails were only available through big-budget-movie special-effects suppliers.

These days, it's easy and affordable to buy a swimmable mermaid tail. Each tail has the same elements of a "skin" that fits tightly from the toes to the

waist, with a "monofin" that you put your feet into. A monofin is the equivalent of two swimming fins fused together, so that your feet look and act like a dolphin's tail fluke.

A MONOFIN IS ESSENTIALLY TWO SWIMMING FINS FUSED INTO ONE SOLID FIN, SIMILAR TO A DOLPHIN'S TAIL FLUKE.

Doreen Virtue, photo © Susan Knight Studios.

A basic mermaid tail for beginners costs between $80 and $250 (U.S. dollars), and is made from spandex, Lycra, or other swimsuit material. More expensive mermaid tails are made from neoprene (wetsuit material), latex, or silicone, which can cost up to $10,000.

You can find ready-made and custom-made mermaid tails for sale on **eBay.com** or through an Internet search for "swimmable mermaid tails." There are tail makers around the world to choose from, and you can read honest consumer reviews on the forum at **mernetwork.com**. Some of the mermaid-tail makers consistently miss their deadlines, or make tails that don't fit well. A quick read of the forum will help you know whom to buy from and whom to avoid. The **mernetwork.com** forum also includes articles about how to make your own swimmable mermaid tail.

If you decide to buy a custom-made tail, I highly recommend having a professional tailor or seamstress take your measurements. Correct measurements are essential to purchasing a mermaid tail that fits you well.

In the following sections, I list the pros and cons of the various materials. (All prices are listed in U.S.

dollars to give you an idea of the costs, but you can buy tails internationally in your own currency.)

Spandex or Lycra Fabric Tails

Price: $80 to $250

Pros: Inexpensive; stretch to accommodate most body sizes; easy to put on and take off; easy to sew, tailor, or decorate; comfortable; available in a variety of colors; easy to rinse off and dry after your swim; lightweight to carry.

Cons: Not very tight fitting and can sag; tend to age fast as they get scraped on the swimming-pool bottom, sand, or ground; photos show the swimmers' legs through the fabric, which makes the tails look unrealistic.

Neoprene Tails

Price: $400 to $8,000

Pros: Moderately priced; stretch to accommodate most body sizes; fairly easy to put on and take off

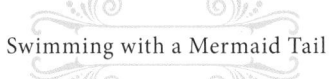

(although not as easy as spandex or Lycra); can accommodate a zipper down the back; fairly easy to sew, tailor, or decorate; provide insulation in cold water; easy to swim in; easy to rinse off and dry after your swim; lightweight to carry.

Cons: Neoprene can tear, pill, or rip easily; limited color choices; chlorine damages the fabric.

Latex Tails

Price: $500 to $2,500

Pros: Realistic looking; provide insulation in cold water; can be tailored on a professional sewing machine; unlimited color choices.

Cons: Difficult to put on and take off; higher priced; may take a long time to make and receive from the manufacturer, as these are generally custom made; can't accommodate a zipper unless it's latex over neoprene; colors scrape off easily against the swimming-pool bottom or ocean sand; heavy to carry.

Silicone Tails

Price $900 to $10,000

Pros: The most realistic looking and feeling; keeps you warm while swimming in cold water; unlimited color choices.

Cons: Expensive; extremely heavy to carry (30 to 60 pounds, but they *are* neutrally buoyant in the water); some are stretchy and easy to put on and take off, while others are tight and difficult to get on and off.

Other factors to consider are the monofins within the tail. Many manufacturers use inexpensive materials and workmanship. Just like cheap shoes that pinch your feet, you get what you pay for with monofins. The straps that go around your ankles should be soft and stretchy, yet strong. Hands down, my favorite monofin is the Finis brand "Competitor" model. It is pricey (around $250 to $300), but in my opinion it's worth every penny. Inexpensive monofins can chafe and cause painful foot and ankle blisters, which take away from the enjoyment of your "mermaiding" swim. The Finis Competitor has a nice blade that makes swimming easy, and the foot

pockets are extremely comfortable (although they run small, and you usually need a size larger than the recommended one).

The Finis Competitor ankle straps are thick and comfortable rubber-band models, so you don't need to fool with buckles, as with most monofins. This is extremely important when putting on a mermaid tail, which requires you to insert your hand through the top opening of the tail while you're in it, and reach down to the monofin at the bottom of the tail. Trying to do that *and* work with buckles is difficult. Another solution is to have a long zipper put in the tail, although only fabric or neoprene tails can accommodate one. True latex (as opposed to latex over neoprene) and silicone tails are too "plastic" to hold a zipper.

What It's Like to Mermaid

The swimmable mermaid-tail phenomenon has expanded the word *mermaid* from a noun to a verb. We now talk about "mermaiding" much like we would "swimming" or "sailing" or another action word. "Mermaiding" means wearing a swimmable mermaid tail and undulating like a dolphin in the ocean or a swimming pool.

I LOVE
SWIMMING
IN MY
MERMAID
TAIL TO
EXPLORE
THE OCEAN'S
BEAUTY.

I've always been drawn to paintings of mermaids, and growing up in coastal Southern California afforded me lots of opportunities to express my inner mermaid by swimming in the ocean and in pools. I took swimming lessons while very young, and I was one of those kids who'd be first in the pool. My mom would have to beg me to come out of it at the end of the day. At the beach, I enjoyed body surfing, swimming, and boogie boarding . . . and just being by the ocean.

As an adult, I became a PADI-certified scuba Dive Master, and went diving a minimum of once a week. I've been scuba diving in the Great Barrier and Osprey reefs of Australia, Tahiti, Mexico, the Caribbean, the Bahamas, Hawaii, and California. I love the feeling of floating weightlessly underwater and being eyeball-to-eyeball with the fish. I had several shark encounters, only one of which was unnerving. I feel completely safe and comfortable underwater. In a way, it feels more like home than when I'm on land.

One day, I was scuba diving in Kona, Hawaii, with my friend the underwater videographer Porter Watson. He told me that before we went on our dive, he had an appointment to "film a mermaid for a documentary." Well, I was intrigued, to say the least!

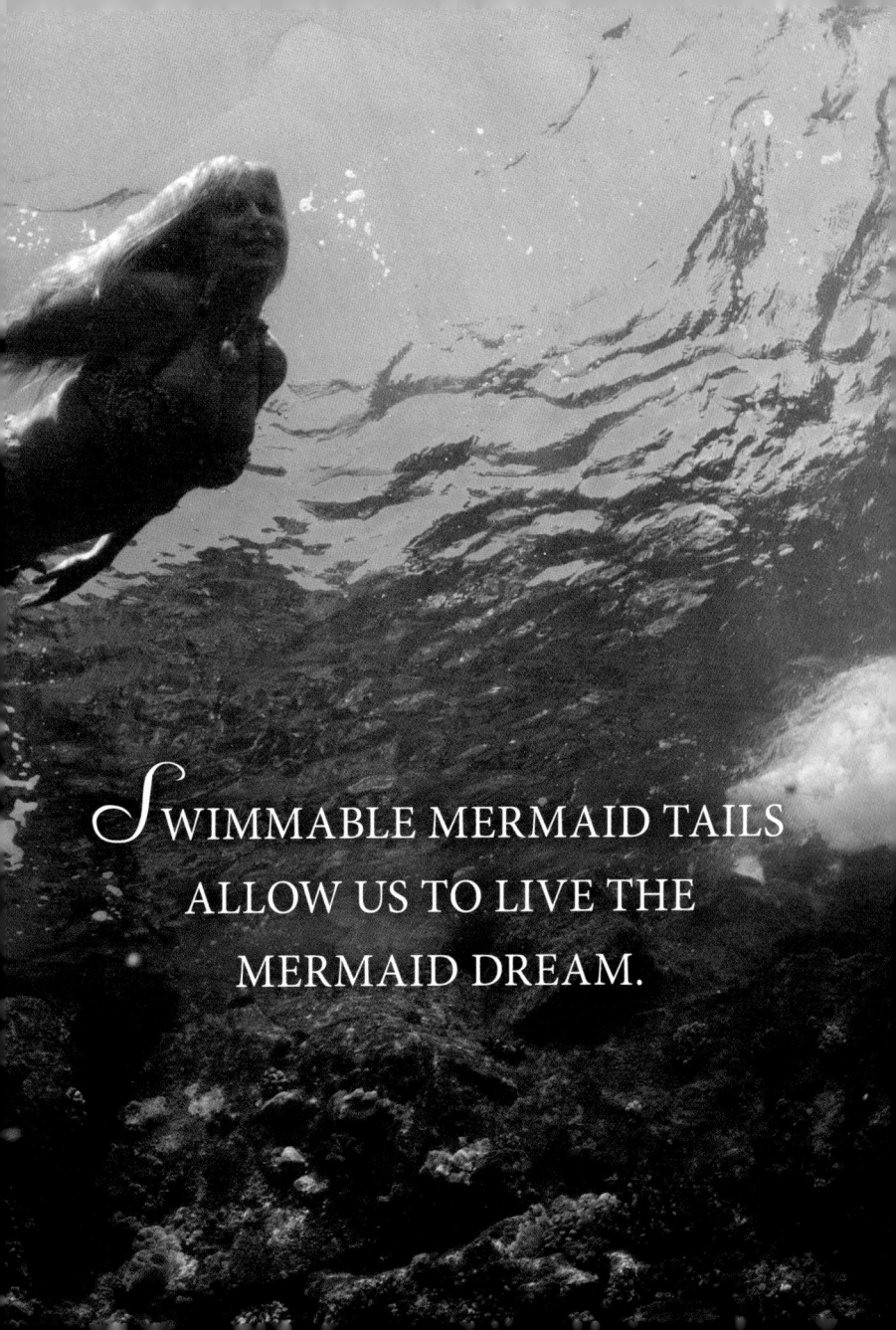

$\int$WIMMABLE MERMAID TAILS
ALLOW US TO LIVE THE
MERMAID DREAM.

A pretty young blonde woman named Dana Richardson was on the beach putting on a neoprene swimmable mermaid tail. I'd previously met Dana on a Kona dolphin-swim boat. I'd been impressed with her ability to free dive deeply with the dolphins. She seemed effortlessly comfortable with these animals, and I was happy to reconnect with her that day.

Dana swam out from shore in her tail, and Porter and I dove beneath the water while he filmed her. As soon as I saw Dana's tail underwater, my heart opened as if I'd seen a real mermaid! The tail she wore was her own creation, with lifelike fins and scales that moved with the water currents. When we surfaced, I asked Dana if she'd consider making a similar tail for me. After a couple of months, she agreed!

The first time I swam with a mermaid tail, I felt a whole new level of connection to the ocean. It took a couple of times before I was accustomed to seeing underwater without goggles or a mask. At first, everything looked like blobs of darkness and light beneath the surface. Today, I can adjust my eyes and see more detail underwater.

Dana and I took a free-diving class along with our friend Susan Knight, "The Mermaid Photographer." The three of us learned how to safely swim

HAVING FUN RE-CREATING THE ICONIC MERMAID ACTION OF BRUSHING MY HAIR UNDERWATER WITH A MIRROR.

COMBINING MY TWO HOBBIES OF PLAYING GUITAR AND MERMAIDING.

deeply on one breath. Through the techniques I learned in class, I was able to remain underwater in a "static breath hold" for nearly four minutes, and I dove to 60 feet on a single breath.

Now that I've been "mermaiding" for several years, I prefer it to scuba diving and any other water activity. It is such an ethereal and beautiful activity that connects us to the ocean in a pure and unadulterated way. I've since introduced a few other girlfriends to mermaiding, and each time I've witnessed them instantly take to it. There's an instinctive ability to undulate like a dolphin underwater. It is pure magic to experience, as a participant and as an observer!

Now let me introduce you to some of my friends who also enjoy mermaiding as an avocation and as a profession. They share inspiring messages about what being a mermaid means to them:

Dana Richardson ("Dana Mermaid")
of Hawaii, Professional Mermaid

"The mermaid is a voice of the sea, and being half fish and half human, she symbolizes our deep connection to the ocean and all sea life. Mermaids are everywhere—some have tails, and some do not. The true meaning of a mermaid lies in her heart, where she holds a pure love for the sea above all else.

"I was born in the desert of Phoenix, Arizona. Much like a fish out of water, I started

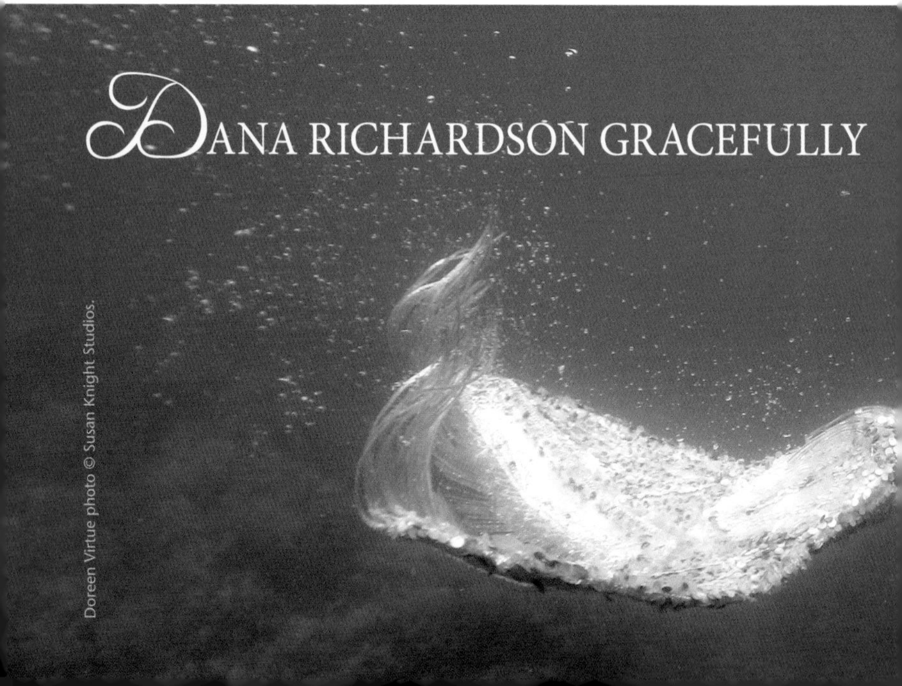

DANA RICHARDSON GRACEFULLY

out in this life very awkward. I learned to swim at a very young age and instinctively felt much more comfortable underwater than on land, a trait that has stayed with me my whole life. I spent much of my early childhood in the swimming pool, and my mom would have to try very hard to get me to come out. I loved the feeling of being in the water and would practice holding my breath underwater and even having underwater tea parties with friends. I would put dive rings around my legs to create a makeshift

GLIDING THROUGH THE WATER

mermaid tail and pretend that I was a real mermaid, and the pool became my outlet to the sea. I would dream of communicating with dolphins and whales.

"I never lost my love for the water or my dreams, but as I reached adolescence, I became much more aware of my awkwardness on land and emotional, sensitive nature. I always felt different from other people and the world where I lived. I moved to Southern California as soon as possible to be near the sea. I will never forget the feeling of having been away from the sea for too long and coming close to a beach and finding the view of the ocean and the smell of the salty air. There are no words to describe this feeling other than 'coming home.'

"As a teenager I struggled a lot with eating disorders and found refuge in drinking. At 19, I admitted I was an alcoholic and started a spiritual path of sobriety. This began my journey to reconnecting to my heart and soul purpose on this planet. After much spiritual work and inner searching, my lifelong dream of communing with dolphins and whales resurfaced, and I found myself

Doreen Virtue photo © Susan Knight Studios.

DANA RICHARDSON SHARES A DEEP BOND WITH THE DOLPHINS.

in Kona, Hawaii, through meditation and prayer guidance. I began working as a crew member on one of the dolphin-swim boats and had many amazing and surreal experiences while taking people swimming with wild dolphins as their safety swimmer and later as a licensed boat captain.

"I've taken paraplegics, kids with cerebral palsy, people with injuries and fears—and even people who don't know how to swim—in with wild dolphins. It's truly touching to

DANA NEXT
TO A HUGE SCHOOL
OF FISH IN HAWAII.

help them face their fears and be comfortable in the sea experiencing the magic and beauty of our dolphin friends.

"I've had amazing encounters with the dolphins and several times have had them rub up against me while swimming. We also play the 'leaf game,' where they pick a leaf up with their rostrum and pass it to their fins or tail or each other and sometimes allow me to share in their game! Dolphins caught in fishing lines allow me to cut it off and free them from the entanglement. I communicate with dolphins through energy and learning their moods and behavior.

"Swimming with dolphins daily for the last 11 years in Kona, I know each of the pods and several by name. Whenever I leave the island and return, I always feel a very big welcome when I see them again. Kona is a very special place, as we have 32 species of whales that live here year-round! The North Pacific humpback whales are protected in Hawaii by the Marine Mammal Protection Act and are our only migrating species swimming through the islands in the winter. French Polynesia is where I journey in the

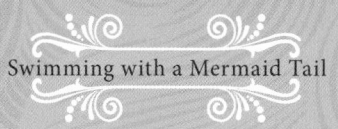
fall to swim with the Southern Pacific humpback whales. The experience of being eye-to-eye underwater with a whale is breathtaking, and no words can express the feelings involved.

"I once came across a humpback whale in Kona that was entangled in a large longline fishing net. I was able to free the whale and pull the net from the sea to prevent another entanglement. One of the most frequent questions I'm asked is: 'Who are the dolphins' and whales' biggest predators?' The answer continues to be *humans*. Through nets, fishing lines, boats, pollution, oil spills, and senseless slaughter in countries that still practice whaling, we as humans are killing species that are considered to be the timekeepers of the sea. Beings as sensitive as we are, with brains larger than the human brain, they deserve our respect and awe.

"Mermaids can be their voices, as there recently was a mass stranding of common dolphins in Peru on Earth Day 2012, which I believe is a call to the human race to wake up and see what we're doing to our ocean, our planet, and ultimately ourselves. This is

$\mathcal{D}$ANA RICHARDSON (IN GOLD) AND ME (IN PINK) ENJOYING UNDERWATER MERMAID FUN.

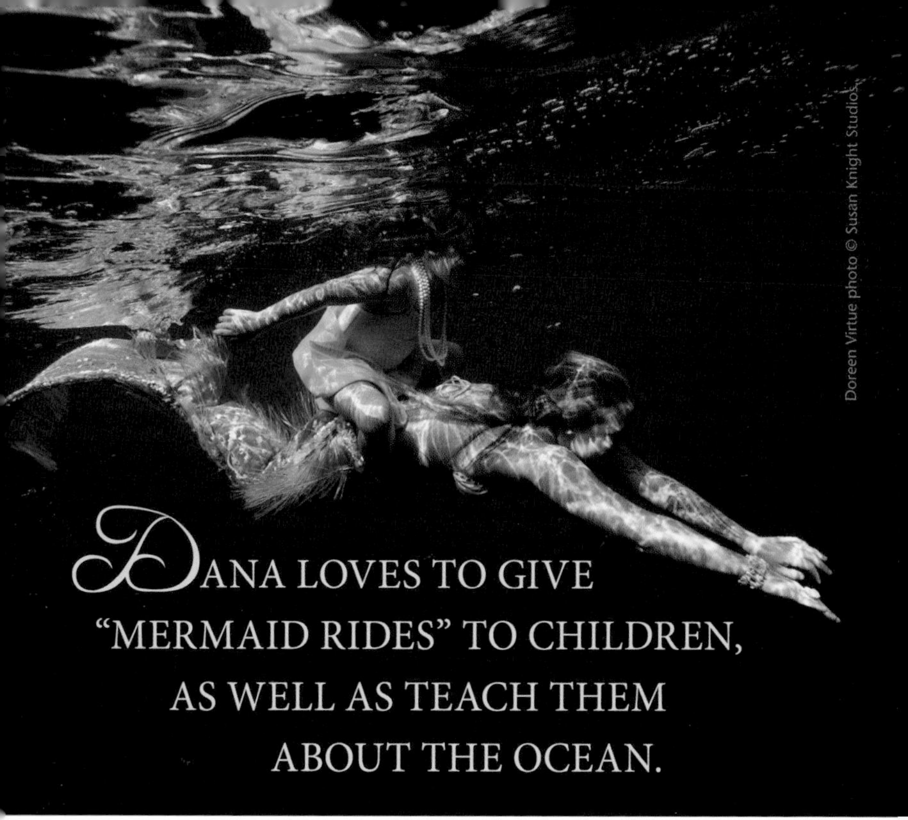

*D*ANA LOVES TO GIVE "MERMAID RIDES" TO CHILDREN, AS WELL AS TEACH THEM ABOUT THE OCEAN.

the mermaid's duty—to show our vital connection to the ocean and all sea life. The dolphins need us . . . and we need them . . . to survive. This is also true of the fish and coral.

"It's so important to learn swim etiquette with wild sea life, including our precious coral reefs. Sunscreen must be put on hours before entering the water to allow it

to absorb into the skin rather than into the reef, which can kill it. It will take hundreds of years for that tiny coral to regrow after it is walked on or even touched.

"Another very large issue right now is plastic bags. These bags will always end up in the sea, and look like jellyfish, which are part of turtles' diet. There is a gyre of floating plastic in the middle of the Pacific Ocean right now, affecting all manner of marine life. In the northwestern Hawaiian Islands, birds and sea life are found dead with plastic lighters inside their bellies from eating the trash found floating in the water.

"One of the biggest things we all can do to help save our oceans is to stop using plastic bags, pick up trash on the beach and in neighborhoods, reuse and recycle items, and learn about the magical world under the sea. Sharks, for example, are creatures that have been feared since the making of the movie *Jaws*. I swim with many species of sharks in the wild and have found them to be very shy and docile creatures who deserve our respect rather than our fear. I believe there is

so much we can learn from the ocean if we just listen.

"My childhood dream of communicating with dolphins and whales and living in the sea has become my reality. If I'm on land too long, my health and mood go down drastically until I can get in the ocean again. One of my main missions is to share my love for the sea and its beauty with the world and help people reconnect to the ocean, our life source, thereby also reconnecting to themselves. The ocean is so healing and has aided in my own transformation of coming home to my soul purpose and being as a mermaid, and I wish to share that with others and speak up for my home, Mother Ocean.

"I began creating and designing swimmable mermaid tails, with 400 to 600 hours going into each one I make. I begin with a vision, and then the tail ends up creating itself, leaving me continually amazed. Each has a different personality on land and under the water.

"The first time I wore a mermaid tail, I felt magical, much like a sea creature, and felt at one with the sea and my dolphin friends. It took my love for the sea to a new

DANA RICHARDSON SILHOUETTED.

and deeper level once I fully decided to jump in with both feet and grow a real tail! It has been a heart-opening and healing journey and evolves constantly as I seek new ways to share my passion and the transformational experience of being a mermaid.

"Doreen Virtue and Susan Knight, our wondrous mermaid photographer, are my sea sisters, and we all recently had the glorious opportunity to share an experience of mermaiding together with the premier ocean artist Wyland. Our mermaid friendship has grown to a much deeper level, and we possess a love for the sea and each other, and a passion to truly help others reconnect to their hearts' purpose.

"I am currently developing transformational mermaid-goddess retreats in Kona and worldwide! I also offer mermaid-swim schools and ocean adventures, have a yearly Dana Mermaid calendar full of inspirational quotes and ocean holidays, as well as a Sea Sister clothing line allowing kids and adults to become mermaid and ocean ambassadors.

"If you have a dream to connect to the ocean on a deeper level or need to reconnect

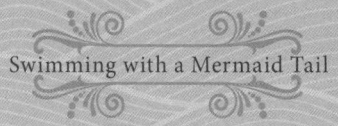
to your heart, or if you envision swimming with dolphins or becoming a mermaid, I would love to share the mer-magic with you! My website is **www.DanaMermaid.com**, and I look forward to swimming with you soon and inspiring your dreams to come true! Fish kisses and starfish wishes from the deep, deep ocean blue! Aloha!"

Susan Knight, "The Mermaid Photographer"

"I was born in western Canada, 22 hours by car away from the nearest ocean. I remember yearning for the sea, before I even knew what it was. I was a landlocked mermaid. That's the way with yearnings, I suppose: they are powerful and draw us to our true path and true selves.

"My journey to the sea began at an early age, as I would sit in my baby seat for hours and watch the fish in our home aquarium. My parents put me in swimming lessons, which I attended regularly for years. To this day, the smell of chlorine makes me feel calm and satisfied, as it represents an early connection to my true element, water. An early-childhood trip to the West Coast was the first time my toes touched the sea. It was magical, and I cried when we had to leave. This same scene was replayed during a trip to Hawaii when I was a teenager.

"As a university student, I became interested in biology and took as many classes about water and water animals as I could, also learning of the amazing properties and qualities of water. At this time, the only exposure I had to marine animals was pickled specimens in jars.

"Struggling somewhat in school, I took time off and went traveling. We all have pivotal times in our lives, and this was one for me. I found myself on the Great Barrier Reef taking my first scuba lesson. It truly is an entirely different world, the world I had been yearning for all these years. I was hooked on scuba. I went back to school to complete my degree, got a job as a lab technician, and spent every weekend training in a murky northern lake. I eventually moved

Susan Knight photo by Rusty Orr.

SUSAN KNIGHT AND HER TRUSTY CAMERA WITH UNDERWATER HOUSING.

to the West Coast to get my scuba-instructor rating. I spent the next 15 years working as a scuba instructor and professional naturalist guide in Canada, the Caribbean, and Hawaii. The teaching curriculum I co-wrote during

$\mathcal{S}$USAN KNIGHT
FREE DIVING
WITH DOLPHINS.

that time is still distributed by PADI (Professional Association of Diving Instructors) and REEF (Reef Environmental Education Foundation). This time was fascinating and combined my love of exploration with the desire to teach others about the ocean.

"Soon afterward, through my work as a model (what mermaid doesn't love fashion?), I fell into several years of film work as a body double, stand-in, and crew member in Canada's 'Hollywood North,' teaching scuba diving part-time. This is where my love of film blossomed, and I became intrigued with photography. At this time, I knew nothing of the art of underwater photography, which would soon become my great love and fascination.

"A trip to Hawaii was another pivotal moment in my journey. I came for a few weeks to the Big Island to take a free-diving course, write, and just be. I met a dive instructor at the shop, and we soon became inseparable. I went back home to finish a film contract and then returned to live in Hawaii with him. We dove, and I learned about photographing underwater. He gifted me my first underwater camera setup, and through his teaching and

the teachings of other great local photographers, I began to feel like an artist.

"It was in the first years in Hawaii that I met Doreen Virtue. I was working on a boat at the time as a scuba-diving guide, and one morning, there she was. Truly a mermaid if ever I saw one! Back in Canada, I'd met with a group of women on a regular basis. We often did readings with various cards, and I was always attracted to Doreen's angel cards. These cards were instrumental in guiding me to Hawaii. I was delighted to meet her, and we soon bonded over our shared love and awe of the ocean world. Eventually, through being involved as a photographer in one of her retreats in Kona, I met Dana Mermaid.

"We met on the boat where she was working as a naturalist, and we were swimming with dolphins. We three began many creative and inspired projects and before I knew it, I had become known as 'The Mermaid Photographer.'

"For me, being a mermaid is about sharing a love and knowledge of the sea with others. I believe the ocean is a part of us, even if some of us have forgotten. I am personally

Susan Knight Mermaiding on the Lava Rock Shores of the Big Island.

Susan Knight photo by Wyland

Susan Knight photo by Wyland.

SUSAN KNIGHT

MERMAIDING DURING OUR WYLAND VIDEO SHOOT.

inspired to help connect people with the sea and water through my work as an underwater portrait photographer.

"It's always exciting and challenging, and that is what keeps me interested. I've left behind much of the scuba gear and transitioned mostly to the freedom of free diving. In the water nearly every day with my camera, I'm exploring and deepening my relationship with the sea. Moving in water, seeing reflections on and around the subjects, and also receiving messages from water is miraculous. So many times, I see things in the editing room that were not apparent during the shoot.

"I recently traveled to Las Vegas for a mermaid convention to photograph people from all over who wear swimmable mermaid tails, several of whom brought their elegant handmade tails. I travel with supplies to set up an instant underwater studio. Many of the mermaids, like me, grew up parched and dry, making their way to the sea. It was wonderful hearing their stories, ironically, sitting around a pool in the middle of the desert.

"While being educated about conservation issues and taking action are important, I also encourage people simply to spend time in nature. Be at the beach, swim in the sea, study anything that interests you about the ocean. Connecting with your true passions and sharing that joyous energy changes the world in dramatic ways. Now is a perfect time to send love and support to the ocean. And remember, mermaids: No matter where you live, you are not alone. We are everywhere."

For underwater portraits and ocean and mermaid images, check out: **www.susanknightstudios. com**.

Hannah Fraser, Model and Professional Mermaid

Hannah Fraser is a passionate ocean activist, and appears regularly to educate audiences on ocean conservation. In 2007, she co-organized a "paddle-out" against dolphin slaughter, during which a

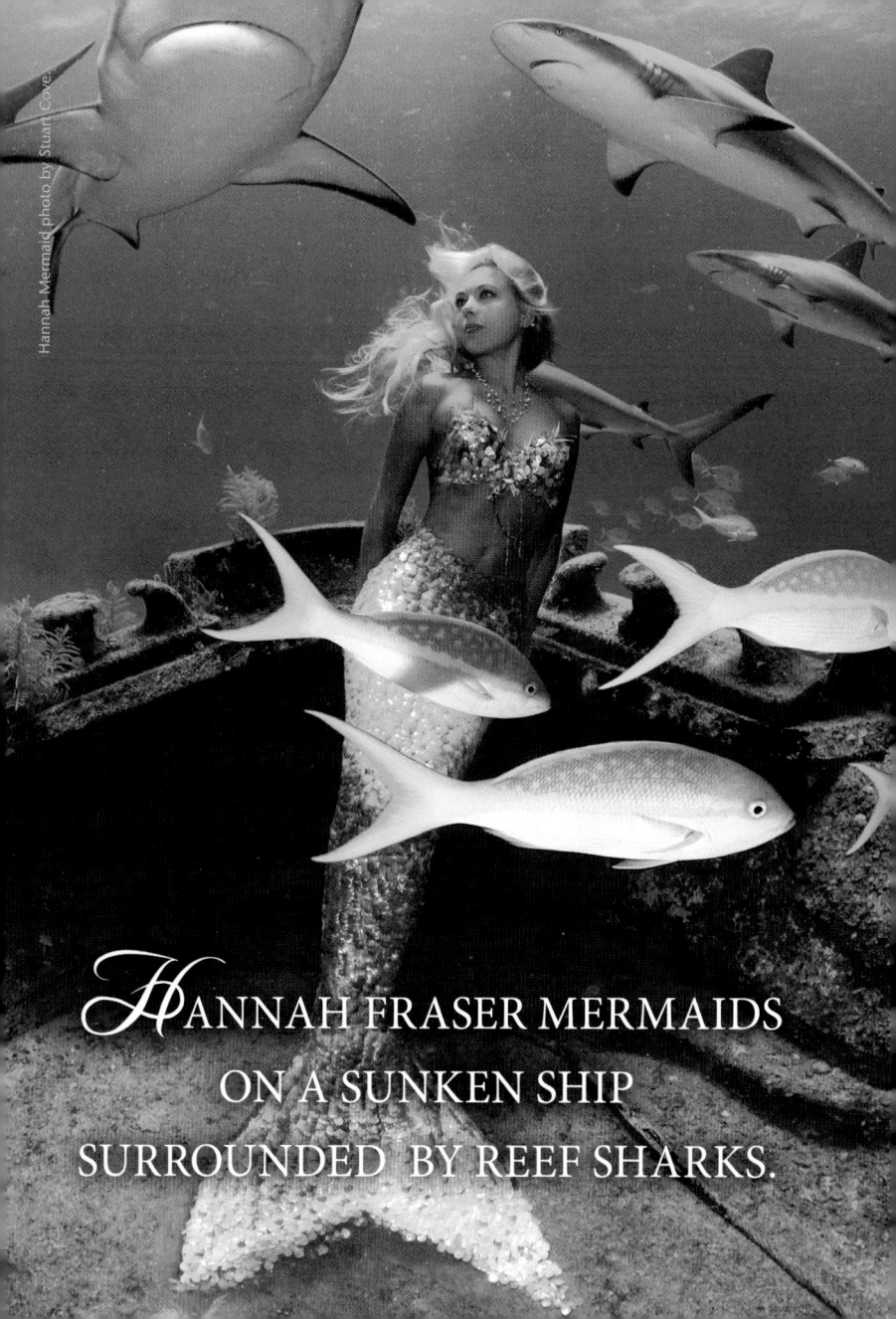

Hannah Mermaid photo by Stuart Cove.

HANNAH FRASER MERMAIDS
ON A SUNKEN SHIP
SURROUNDED BY REEF SHARKS.

HANNAH FRASER
IS A PASSIONATE
OCEAN ADVOCATE.

Hannah Mermaid photo by James Vu.

group of activists attempted to shield dolphins from being killed in Taiji, Japan. This became one of the first actions to raise attention on dolphin killings in Japan and was later featured in the Oscar-winning documentary *The Cove*. Hannah has also appeared on the television shows *20/20*, *Nightline*, and *Good Morning America*.

"The ocean is our lifeblood. If we mess it up with pollution, overfishing, and killing these incredible species that hold the knowledge and the wisdom of the ocean, it's only a matter of years before the rest of civilization crumbles. We can't survive without the ocean. It's the womb of the world. We are 70 percent water. We can no longer pretend that we're just these land-based creatures and that we don't have a completely symbiotic relationship with the ocean.

"I think people are attracted to mermaids because they represent our connection to the ocean, which is the womb of all life! Mermaids are the 'known' human form (represented in its most alluring beautiful female vision) and then a fish tail, which is representative of the 'unknown' . . . the

depths of the sea, and Mother Nature in all her awesome glory.

"I think the stories of sirens calling sailors to drown in the depths of the ocean is a metaphor for humans surrendering to their own depths of emotion, and the great unknown. It can be interpreted as a positive 'letting go' into the deep wisdom of nature. A death of our imperialistic way of thinking that we are separate from our surroundings, instead of the reality of our symbiotic relationship with the earth.

"I think people want to integrate with nature in new ways. They don't just want to scuba dive in a cumbersome suit that feels limiting and separate from the underwater world. They want to play in the ocean like they are part of it—one of its creatures that belongs there—not just a spectator but an interactive creature.

"Being a mermaid gives me a firsthand perspective of what is going on in the ocean in different parts of the world. I have swum in the most beautiful pristine locations and also ones with the most polluted and rubbish-filled beaches. It breaks my heart to see

HANNAH FRASER INSPIRES
OTHERS TO LIVE THEIR DREAMS.

the degradation, so I feel I need to help with the mess we have created in our lust for commercialism and our 'throwaway' culture. I help promote sustainable lifestyles, eat only vegetarian and organic food at every opportunity, support ocean-conservation organizations, and utilize my mermaid persona to inspire people to connect to the underwater world and care about the amazing creatures who reside within it.

"My whole life all I ever wanted to do was inspire people to live their dreams, whatever they may be. I want to show people that if they are continually passionate about what they believe in, anything is possible!

"I'm completely re-inspired every day by seeing other people who have the same passion and who've been awakened to the beauty of the ocean like that."

Hannah's website is **hannahmermaid.com**.

Linden Wolbert, Professional Mermaid
and Free Diver

Linden Wolbert has always felt most comfortable and happy in the water. Competitive swimming as a child led to a passion for snorkeling, scuba diving, and free diving, taking her around the globe to explore seas and pools and all creatures great and small. With a B.A. in Film and Science from Emerson College in Boston, Linden has knowledge both behind and in front of the camera that has proved invaluable in her aquatic pursuits. A professional underwater model, videographer, and avid diver living in Los Angeles, she hopes to reach, inspire, and educate others—especially children—about ocean conservation and water safety through her unusual line of work. Mermaid Linden has been featured in countless magazines; in online publications; and on news programs on ABC, NBC, the Oprah Winfrey Network, and beyond. She can be seen diving her way through PADI scuba-agency educational materials and working as an ambassador for Reef Check worldwide.

Linden Wolbert photo © mermaidsinmotion.com.

$\mathcal{L}$INDEN WOLBERT HOPES TO INSPIRE OTHERS, ESPECIALLY CHILDREN, ABOUT WATER CONSERVATION THROUGH HER MERMAID WORK.

"Being a mermaid is the most transcendental feeling I have ever experienced. Suspended in the ocean's colors of blue and green, enveloped by warm, clear water, it's a sensation unlike anything else on Earth. To be a mermaid is to be a creature of the sea. It evokes a unique sense of complete adaptation one cannot sense in scuba gear, although I adore scuba diving for different reasons. In this swaying, slow-motion environment, I am weightless and unencumbered. Fish dance and play around me, sea fans sway in the ocean current, and it is very quiet . . . so quiet that I can hear my own heartbeat. Sometimes I hear the crackle of the animals on the reef, nibbling away on food with an array of clicks and chatter. I crave the infinitely peaceful sensation I feel when I am in the water.

"The beauty of the sea, its delicate balance, and what it offers to our planet inspire me to no end. It is such a nurturing, fascinating, ever-changing place. If you look at just a square inch of a coral reef, you will see a microcosm of life existing in that space, like a small underwater city: The starfish crawls

slowly across the ocean floor and bumps into a stingray who rests silently under the sand . . . and above them an eel weaves through the crags and cracks of the coral, mouth agape, with a cleaner shrimp performing delicate dental work in perfect symbiosis. The Christmas tree worm is startled by this movement and disappears in a blink, retreating into its home, and cautiously reaches out its colorful, feathery display a few moments later. These are all things observed on breath hold on the reef.

"Breath-hold diving, or free diving, is a huge part of my career as a mermaid and my recreational life. I was inspired to design and create my 35-pound prosthetic silicone mermaid tail the first time I saw a competitive monofin, which is a single fin with two foot pockets. As an international judge for the sport of free diving, I am privileged to have a front-row seat to the performances of the deepest divers in the world. Currently, my personal best depth on a single breath of air is 35 meters (114 feet) and back up again. I have a static breath hold of five minutes. I must stress that this is a result of professional

Linden Wolbert photo © Matthew Douglas Addison Photography.

*L*INDEN WOLBERT SAYS THAT BEING A MERMAID IS THE MOST TRANSCENDENTAL FEELING SHE'S EVER EXPERIENCED.

129

training, extreme caution, and the presence of safety divers with me at all times. If you take one thing from this paragraph, please remember *never to dive or practice breath hold alone.* With proper safety protocols in place, free diving is a very safe and enjoyable way to experience the big blue!

"My heart's true calling is to share the ocean with children and encourage them to experience it for themselves and to become ambassadors of the most vital 70 percent of our blue planet. Since my own fascination with the ocean began at a tender age, I feel this is the perfect time to plant the seed of conservation in a child's heart. I call these children my "little sea fans"! When youngsters fall in love with something, they are very protective of it. They share it with their friends. Personal interaction with the ocean and its inhabitants is the perfect way to create a sense of responsibility for our oceans.

In my children's ocean education series, *Mermaid Minute,* kids have the opportunity to learn about specific creatures, habitats, and phenomena in the ocean. Sending these messages through the vessel of a mermaid

Linden Wolbert photo © Agustin Munoz.

$\mathcal{M}$ERMAID LINDEN TEACHES CHILDREN TO TAKE PERSONAL RESPONSIBILITY FOR THE OCEAN'S HEALTH.

131

makes a memorable and magical impact on them. When I am in the water with children, I am as delighted and enchanted as they are! Making a difference in a child's view of our oceans is an incredible gift. I am overwhelmed with happiness in my line of work, and cannot imagine doing anything but mermaiding!"

In 2011, Linden dreamed up and created her original series, *Mermaid Minute,* with the wish that any child may have access to ocean-education programming that teaches him or her to explore, love, and protect our oceans! Learn more about the series at: **www.mermaidminute.com**. Mermaid Linden performs worldwide for special events, fund-raisers, and nonprofit galas to help kids and older humans learn how they impact our oceans. To hire her or learn more about her life as a professional mermaid, please visit: **www.mermaidsinmotion.com**.

CHAPTER EIGHT

MERMAID VISIONS AND DREAMS

I first wrote about mermaids in my 2001 book *Healing with the Fairies*, in which I described being at the ocean's edge and seeing a vision of a mermaid in the surf mist. She conveyed to me a great feeling of peaceful love, and an appeal to join her. There was a familiarity about her that triggered deep memories and further stirred my ocean activism activities.

Since that time, I've received many letters from readers who have also connected with the spiritual

energy of mermaids. I've included a few of their stories for you to enjoy and learn from here. . . .

It was 1993, and Kathleen and her closest friends were taking an energy-balancing course. The bodywork helped clear their energy fields of any painful, traumatic experiences they might have been carrying. It also helped balance their physical, mental, emotional, and spiritual bodies to assist them in aligning with the new energies of light that were coming onto the planet—a light that promised peace, happiness, abundance, and good health for all.

It was the last class, and a few individuals had been working with Kathleen's energy field. Afterward, she relaxed peacefully on the massage table, bathed in a beautiful, glowing light. That's when it happened! She energetically morphed into a beautiful mermaid with long, flowing hair. Her body from the waist down was a shimmering dark green sheath, mixed with some patterns of brown and blue, which wrapped around her where her legs would have been.

She looked up and saw a wide, perfectly shaped finlike tail, and around her neck were strings of flowers, shells, and colored stones. Kathleen was aware

that she inhabited a watery world full of sunlight and purity, a place not of this earth. Her heart was satisfied, content, and full of the essence of her life. She was loved by the sun and water, and she delighted in all existence. Then the experience dissolved back into light, leaving her with an awakened memory.

About ten years later, Kathleen came upon my book *Earth Angels* and read descriptions of what she always felt herself to be. Many characteristics of an Incarnated Angel coincided with her memories of star ancestors. I had mentioned the Merangel, a light being that was evolving, and Kathleen related to that.

In this life, she loves to collect shiny things and keep them in "treasure boxes." When she was young, she would delight in swimming in the ocean with her feet crossed, spinning round and round in the waves. That simple act filled her with joy.

Recently, Kathleen has been reconnecting with the mermaid part of her being. She has a memory of bringing forth sound frequencies to help balance and purify her environment. She also participates in a teleconferencing group every morning, and sings soul songs for Mother Earth. She always directs these energies into the Pacific Ocean for the dolphins and the whales.

In the film *Pirates of the Caribbean: On Stranger Tides,* there's a story about needing a mermaid's tears to help a person live forever. Kathleen cries many tears anytime there is willful destruction of the beauty of Mother Earth and all her beloved creatures, but it would be sad to think she has to cry forever. She would like to see this story turned around, and mermaids and other magical creatures spin and laugh and sing so that they could help bring about Heaven on Earth.

Kathleen knows deep in her heart that all beings are loved by the Divine.

Growing up, Lynn Hohengarten always spent as much time in the water as possible. But since she lived on the East Coast, in Connecticut, that meant she could only enjoy this pastime about three months out of the year. She remembers that as a child, she always stayed in the water much longer than any of her friends. When they would practice holding their breath underwater, she'd be beneath the surface actually trying to breathe. She thought that if she drew the water into her mouth, she could "suck out" the air particles that she needed, and then expel the rest.

Her family used to joke that she was somewhat of a klutz, always tripping, falling, or bumping into things. But the minute she got into the water, while *they* would be thrashing around, there she was, gliding through the water like she was born to it.

Years later, while vacationing in Rockport, Massachusetts, a charming artists' colony on the coast, Lynn found a painting of a mermaid that intrigued her. She bought it because the mermaid wasn't sitting on a rock, or above water at all. She was sitting underwater, perfectly happy. This was the beginning of her affinity with mermaids.

After she got married and became pregnant, Lynn went to Lamaze classes. The women there were supposed to visualize, and concentrate on, a calm place. Afterward, everyone was asking one another what they'd envisioned. There was a lot of "at the beach" or "at the lake" or "lying on the grass under a tree." But Lynn was the only one who saw herself underwater. Everyone thought that was a little odd.

A few years ago, Lynn attended a mind-body expo in her city. There were mediums and clairvoyants and people who would pull cards from a deck and answer questions. She sat down at one woman's table and asked for a card reading. Now she had never met this woman, and Lynn wasn't wearing a

sea-glass necklace or anything ocean related, nor was she even wearing anything blue. There was nothing in her dress or demeanor that would have given the reader a clue as to Lynn's affinity with water.

The woman had many different types of cards on her table—angel decks, fairy decks, animal decks, and so on. So what did she do? She went directly to my *Magical Mermaids and Dolphins Oracle Cards* and told Lynn, "I think this is the deck for you."

You could have knocked Lynn over with a feather. She had never seen those cards before and didn't even know that such a deck existed. Then the woman had Lynn pull a few cards. One of them was a replica of a painting by artist Jim Warren. It was called "Friendship" and depicted a mermaid tea party. Lynn stared at the card and then at the woman and started to get teary eyed. The reader asked her what was wrong, and she replied, "I just pulled a card of an actual painting that's hanging in my dining room!" The reader was just as amazed as Lynn was.

Lynn has now been living in Florida for the past 22 years, and she is probably in some kind of water—ocean, river, spring, or pool—nine or ten months out of the year. She has her scuba certification and has been diving all over Florida, Mexico, California, and

the Caribbean. Sometimes when she has her gear on underwater, she doesn't even swim around. She just sinks to the bottom and sits there. It's the best feeling in the world.

Andrea had a mermaid dream that took place along a beach on a windy day at sunset. She was looking out toward the ocean from her seaside condo when she noticed a yellow floppy hat, trimmed with yellow roses, floating from the condo's roof onto the ocean waves. She recognized the hat as hers, and in both wonder and disgust, she ran out to save it from the deep, even though it was now dusk.

As she was running into the waves, Andrea heard female laughter. She could almost hear her name being called or sung. Then she saw three mermaids playing in the water. She couldn't see a lot of detail, but all three had long hair, and the water was glittery and soft-looking around them. Even though she had good feelings watching the mermaids, her mind raced with indecision. "Am I an intruder, or am I welcome?" She decided to turn around and get her hat and go back to the condo.

As she was swimming back to shore, she heard a very loud rushing wind or waterfall-type noise behind her. She looked back, and a baby humpback whale was swimming up behind her. Out of the corner of her eye, she could still see the three mermaids watching and laughing. The baby whale rolled over for her to rub his tummy, and she thought, *I've got to get out of his way!* and proceeded to dive underwater. As she torpedoed toward the shore, she woke up.

Andrea isn't sure of the significance of the dream . . . but it has helped her be aware of the importance of sound for healing purposes.

Nadine recently had a fascinating vision about mermaids. It revealed how the Atlanteans used to swim like these lovely sea creatures to help them move easily through water. The angels showed Nadine that the sailors saw the Atlanteans resting on rocks in their swimming gear, and mistook them for actual mermaids. She believes that the Atlanteans used the mermaids' technique of swimming to move through the water more effectively. They could swim faster and more naturally, much like the

mermaids themselves. Who knows, they may have even been friends!

She also gets the sense that mermaids were much more abundant in the sea during this time—that is, in that ancient era, they were a thriving part of ocean life. Now she feels that they're hidden, isolated, or few in number. But she can't say that they're no longer on this planet. She knows that their spirits live on because she can still feel them here, and believes that they reside in the sea.

Nadine prays that the mermaids' world becomes a safe one so that they can come out and play like they did in ancient times . . . and that humans, just like the ancient Atlanteans, can explore the magic of the oceans with these fascinating and beautiful sea maidens.

What does a rock in a semidesert setting have to do with a mermaid, the famed lady of the water? The answer comes from the most unexpected place—the heart of the South African region called the Karoo.

Jodi Rogers always had a strong connection with nature. Her childhood was filled with memories of running free outdoors, roaming in the veld

collecting wildflowers and quartz crystals, or simply sitting at the top of a hill while watching the world go by. Of these memories, her favorite times are those spent by the sea. The ocean was and is her spiritual home. Even during the colder months, just being able to walk on the beach as the sand molded the memory of her presence into each footprint was enough. Being there, she felt her soul dance to the rhythm of the waves, and the ocean breeze whisper sacred secrets in her ears. She would close her eyes and walk along the shore, with the water gently washing up over her feet. The sound of the crashing surf and wind filled her with nervous excitement as she allowed her inner compass to guide her step-by-step.

After graduating from a university in South Africa, Jodi moved inland to the big city of Johannesburg in search of employment. This was a huge adjustment. Although she eventually got used to it, periodically she was overcome by a longing to retreat to the seaside. For the most part, it was bearable, since she made a trip to the coast at least twice a year. However, about five years ago, she gained new insight into this longing. At the time, she was undergoing a period of spiritual growth, and was drawn to crystal and color healing. She'd just gotten her own

set of crystals and started to incorporate crystal healing in her meditation. After a few weeks of doing so, her meditation began to deepen, and her sensitivity increased. Her dreams became more vivid.

One night Jodi had a dream that left a potent residual impression on her. She dreamed that she had long light brown hair and wore a pale blue robe. There was an old man standing on her right-hand side. He wore a long white robe with silver trim and a silver rope around his waist. From his air of wisdom, she knew that he was her teacher. They were in the middle of an abandoned stone town of some sort, and there were no other people in sight, but Jodi felt that there was someone else with them. When she looked to see who it was, she saw a dolphin in a water channel that meandered through the town. Jodi felt a profound sense of companionship with this dolphin.

With a sense of urgency, she and her teacher ran along a stone pathway with the dolphin swimming through the channel beside them. They eventually reached a courtyard full of beautiful mermaid sculptures. Jodi was taken by the beauty of the artwork. Looking at the building they were running toward, they saw that its big, heavy wooden doors were closed. They knew that it was too late. They

were meant to be *inside* the building. Some of the other stone buildings in the town started crumbling as the floodwaters rose higher and higher. It also struck Jodi that throughout the dream, not a word was spoken. She seemed to be communicating with her teacher and the dolphin telepathically.

After that night, the images of the mermaid statues remained vividly in Jodi's mind, which inspired her to find out more about mermaids. She devoured any information she could find. The first deck that she purchased was my *Magical Mermaids and Dolphins Oracle Cards*. They became a refreshing source of comfort and daily guidance for her. The idea of mermaids being associated with people who were involved in environmentalism resonated with Jodi's experience, since she worked in that field.

The deeper she looked, the more she found. She discovered the links between dolphins, mermaids, and Atlantis. The details that she unraveled seemed to put her dream into context bit by bit, and the experience inspired her to write poetry about mermaids. At work, she often found herself doodling and drawing the profile of a mermaid. She learned that both crystal and color healing were associated with Atlantis, and it was clearly no coincidence that her dream, as well as her fascination with mermaids,

was sparked when she began working with these forms of healing.

Jodie had a number of other dreams where she walked among the mermaid statues. She was a little confused that the descriptions of Atlantis, although close, didn't quite match the architecture in her dreams. She later learned that other antediluvian civilizations may have existed, which made her feel that the place in her dreams may have been one of those locales.

Of all the information that Jodi has gathered about mermaids, the most fascinating stories have been the ones close to home. She first heard of an African link to mermaids from a story her mother-in-law told her about Mermaid's Pool in Zimbabwe. This place got its name because over the years, many of the local people claimed that they'd spotted pale-skinned women with dark stringy hair in the water. That particular part of the story stuck in her mind because she'd first heard it from her grandmother, a Shona woman who didn't speak much English yet used the word *mermaid*. What's interesting about this is that the sightings of the legendary water beings at Mermaid's Pool date back before contact with European explorers and colonizers. Jodi knew of many Zimbabwean and South African folklore

stories that spoke of water spirits, but it was the first time someone had mentioned mermaids.

Intrigued, Jodi set about to find out if there were any original South African stories of mermaids prior to contact with European settlers as well. Coincidentally, while on a flight to Cape Town, she was sitting in the window seat marveling at the vast land below. She was sure the plane must have been flying over the Karoo because she could hardly see any signs of development.

The Karoo is a semiarid part of the country that stretches across vast portions of the central interior. The ancient San hunter-gatherer tribes roamed these lands for thousands of years before any European settlers set foot in South Africa. These dry and desolate landscapes emanate an air of antiquity, and the energy in this ancient place is alive with mystery.

Captivated by the idea of the Karoo, Jodi picked up the in-flight magazine and stumbled across an article about the very place she'd just been thinking of. What's more, the article was about a woman who was making a documentary about mermaids in the Karoo. The Klein Karoo area (Little Karoo) is known for stories of water beings that the locals call *watermeid,* or water maidens. These mystical beings are half fish and half human, just like mermaids.

According to the stories, these maidens are spirits of the water who live in the springs of the ravines and mountainous parts of the southern Karoo. Local people in this area who believe in their existence have viewed them suspiciously for centuries. Water maidens are thought to be protective of their water holes and springs, and sometimes dangerous. They have magical powers and can control the weather and the rain. There are various stories of people who were pulled under by these water beings and who spent a short time living underwater with them. Accounts from early settlers show that these stories existed before their arrival.

So where do these tales come from? Whatever the answer is, one thing that's clear is that the idea of mermaids in the Klein Karoo has been around a lot longer than many people might have imagined. Jodi was completely stunned to discover paintings of mermaids featured in the rock art in this area, which dates back thousands of years. There's something amazing about the connection with the past that they provide. Ancient people transcribed images on rocks to pass on an element of themselves to future generations. Jodi believes that she is part of that future generation, and sometimes feels like this art is a personal letter from the mermaids to her.

And in moments when she doesn't know where she's going in life, she thinks about that, and it comforts her, because she knows that thousands of years ago, the mermaids anticipated that she would be here.

The mermaid rock art occurs close to deep water holes and reservoirs. It is likely that the stories associated with these paintings were passed on from generation to generation, and are, hence, alive today. People in the area still report mermaid sightings. Interestingly, approximately 250 million years ago, the Karoo was under the sea. Many people still find seashells in the middle of this semidesert landscape. Perhaps it still radiates the vibration of the ocean.

Sara Gonzalez, a woman who hails from Las Vegas, is an incarnated mermaid from the desert. Through dreams, visions, and incredibly powerful channelings, this beautiful knowledge has been confirmed many times—to the point where she has been put under hypnosis and has experienced past-life regressions to the mer-world. This has helped her better understand her current life.

Sara strongly feels that one of her soul missions is to bring the energy from the mer-world into her

art and poetry. When she draws these visions of the mermaids, she sees sparks of blue, purple, and white light on the paintings or on her hands. She feels guided by the angels and mermaids to channel information to disseminate to the public. It's been wonderful! She's been involved in the spiritual path for a long time now, and seeing visions from these realms has been truly fascinating.

Sara believes that knowing who you are on such a deep level is important to one's spiritual growth, and she truly thinks that this is one of the lessons she is bringing to others in this lifetime. Many of the situations she is in now relate very much to the mermaid life from so long ago. She believes that the mermaids are around her quite often, and sees them through her third eye. They are incredibly beautiful. She has even met many other incarnated mermaids, and some mermen as well, who are quite conscious of their origins. They too have talents to share and are very creative. Sara believes this energy, if chosen, should be shared to uplift Mother Earth, which many are doing. This is truly a blessing, and she really hopes to bring peace and love through her God-given talents to the world. She knows that art holds a sacred energy that can be imprinted on Earth to give love, healing, and wisdom.

When Cora Flora was a little girl, she absolutely adored swimming. She loved to pretend she was a mermaid, and always felt a connection to these angels of the water. A few years ago, she was going through a challenging time in her life, and her heart kept guiding her to go to the water and write. Every day she would head to the beach, swim, lie in the sun, and write streams of inspiration as they flowed through her.

Cora felt herself connecting with the spirit of the mermaids, and beautiful underwater stories began to emerge. Woven into the accounts were intuitive symbols of mermaid wisdom, including guidance for embracing sexual energy and using singing as a tool for healing. Her first book, *Marla the Mermaiden,* helped her understand what she was going through and how to transcend the illusions of limitation in her life. The book helped her remember that life is truly here to support her, for her highest good.

Since Cora wrote that work, many of those intuitive symbols have been keys to unlocking healing wisdom and power in her life. She has been through a deep journey of healing from sexual abuse, and is now at the point of embracing her body and its

beautiful sexual energy as the spiritual power it is. She is also a musician, and her underwater adventures have helped her tune in to deeper levels of emotional resonance, as well as rediscover the power of sound. She now leads workshops about this topic, and also shows people how to sing from the soul.

Cora definitely believes in mermaids, and during a past-life regression she was taken back to a life where *she* was one of these delightful sea creatures, full of wisdom and deep music. Remembering this has helped her be the juicy, deep, and sensual woman she is today!

Jessica was in a group of people doing a spirit assembly when she "saw" that they were all underwater, and others were seeing this, too. All of a sudden, she was seeing a beautiful female mermaid in front of her with thick, flowing hair. The mermaid was holding a shell out in front of her, and inside it was a pearl. The mermaid handed Jessica the shell and pearl and gave her the message that she holds the "pearls of wisdom" in her hands. Then she swam away. It was an amazing and beautiful experience!

It was the middle of July, and Lacey Jackson had rented an apartment for a month in Port Townsend, Washington, a small town in between the Olympic Mountains and Puget Sound. She wanted to take a break from her everyday routine so she could figure out what was next in her life. One thing she knew was that she was ready for a change.

A few weeks later, Lacey was having lunch with a girlfriend in Tacoma; after eating, they decided to walk along the waterfront. There was a small section of logs and a patch of sand along the path, so they decided to sit down. As they were hanging out, they noticed a bright pink object along the water line. Lacey's friend picked it up and said, "This is surely for you, Lacey." It was a little doll with long pink hair. Her two legs were so close together that it looked as if she could definitely turn into a mermaid if she went into the water. Lacey and her friend both laughed in delight. Over their lunch, Lacey had told her friend of her lifelong affinity with mermaids, and the fact that she'd always believed in them.

As the days passed, mermaids kept showing up in Lacey's life. One day she went into a tea shop near her apartment and noticed several mermaids hanging on the wall. They were made out of rawhide and

decorated with beads and seashells. She fell in love with them.

One event occurred after another relating to these magnificent sea creatures. Lacey was thinking about doing intuitive readings, and a friend directed her to a store called Mystical Mermaid. When she called the establishment, a very cheerful young man's voice answered. Lacey introduced herself and told him that she wanted to do intuitive readings somewhere.

The way he responded made her start jumping up and down, and she knew that he was doing the same on the other end of the phone. He and his wife had just put out feelers for someone to do readings in their store, which they had bought a few months before. They had followed their dream of raising their four kids somewhere other than the city, and had bought the Mystical Mermaid boutique and had turned it a metaphysical store with lots of mermaid trinkets.

The mermaids were definitely helping Lacey as she progressed on her path. She met new friends, started doing work she loved, and took more time to write. And she was assured by the mermaids that her life would just get better and better. She even met a friend on a dating site who's a seaweed expert, and

helped her formulate a scrub-and-masque product that she will sell at Mystical Mermaid.

She has been told by an islander that the area where she lives is where Lemuria was located. The islands hold an incredible amount of wonder. When Lacey looks over at the trees across the bay, there's a dragon and a wizard with a big wand that greets her every day. Her life just keeps getting more and more magical.

Being a Pisces, Coventina Waterhawk always identified with the sign of the fish. She even has a large tattoo of a mermaid with a dolphin on her lower leg. Not too long ago, she had an experience that led to a profound spiritual awakening with a specific mermaid.

Coventina had been psychic since childhood, but she suppressed her gifts until December 2001, when they were reawakened the first night of a Tarot reading class. She did her first one-card reading with a woman she didn't know, and she was so accurate that it stunned not only her, but everyone in the class. The attendees were convinced that she should do readings for a living.

In 2006, she started to conduct readings at a metaphysical store, whose owner happened to be a practitioner certified by me (Doreen). It was at this time that Coventina read my book *Earth Angels* and identified with the Wise Ones as well as the Elementals. And then after reading my book *Realms of the Earth Angels,* she found herself identifying as an Incarnated Merfairy. The fairies are constantly yelling in her ears, making sure she picks up litter in public, and she becomes infuriated when she sees people snuff out cigarettes on the ground or toss them into the street. She immediately goes up to them and asks, "Excuse me, would you put that cigarette out on your living-room rug?" When they respond "No," she says, "Well, then, please don't put it out on the Mother's belly." They usually apologize and pick it up and throw it in the trash. She also keeps fairy dust with her at all times to sprinkle onto others for blessings.

Being an intuitive healer has led Coventina to offer several unique services to her clients. She combines Reiki & Readings—"R&R"—and conducts parties for large groups. She has been a party animal her entire life, so these events are her favorite. She is always the first one there and the last one to leave. She has become so spiritually intoxicated that she

has to be extra careful driving home, though. She has missed her freeway exit on occasion.

Since she embarked on the path of helping others, remarkable healings have taken place in Coventina's own life: spiritually, mentally, emotionally, and physically. Ten years ago, she resonated with a Celtic goddess but had forgotten all about her. This led up to her recent experience:

One day, this goddess returned with an overwhelming energy that Coventina had not felt for quite some time. Having had spiritual experiences and awakenings before, she knew what was happening but was perplexed by the goddess's use of her name. The goddess's voice got louder, and her energy was increasing from within her and around her until Coventina surrendered to her and voiced out loud: "My name is Coventina!"

This conviction resonated in the depths of her soul, and a warm, electric current went through her entire body, surrounding her whole being. She almost felt like a "walk-in" because the shift was so sudden. She immediately created a new Facebook profile with her new name: "Coventina Waterhawk."

Waterhawk has been her magical name since 2001. She looked up the meaning, and the first description was a Celtic river goddess known for

healing! When Coventina told her friends what the name represented, they said, "That's you!" Some friends then nicknamed her "Covie," which resonated with the fairy aspect of who she is. When others asked why she changed her name, she told them that she *didn't* change her name; her name changed *her.* The name Coventina is also associated with renewal, abundance, new beginnings, life cycles, inspiration, childbirth, wishes, prophecy, and divination.

Coventina is currently in the process of legally changing her name, and is looking forward to seeing it, along with her photo, on her driver's license and passport.

Sheelin is a "Merfairy." She lives on San Juan Island, Washington, and her passion is beachcombing. She is happiest at the beach or in the water (Hawaiian ocean water preferably, but hot sea-salt baths work well, too!). The beach, the sound of the waves, and the heavenly scents make it feel like a sacred place for her.

Sheelin had a collection of sea glass from her beach adventures, and she thought the smooth, frosted pastel glass pieces would make gorgeous gems

to wear. This was an original idea to her, and she thought of it long before sea glass became so popular. She started selling her sea-glass jewelry in 1995.

One night Sheelin had a very vivid dream. In it, her husband took her to a beach where there were three coves. The first cove was the longest, and then there was a small one, and then a medium-size one. The scenery was breathtaking, and everywhere there was sea glass in all shades of aqua, green, lavender, and cobalt blue. It was such a wonderful feeling.

A few days after the dream, her husband, who had previously been a surfer in Hawaii, said to her, "I have a new friend, and he said we can go down to his private beach and beachcomb." When they arrived at the beach, Sheelin was shocked. It was exactly the same beach she'd seen in her dream—with the three coves and tons of colored sea glass, all perfectly frosted and smooth.

It was then and there that Sheelin first heard the mermaids speaking to her. She heard voices in her head, but not her own. One day she got very specific instructions: "Go over to that big log on the sand, take three steps to the right, and turn over the green leaf." She thought, *This is really weird,* but she did what the voice told her.

Underneath the leaf was a magnificent aqua bottle stopper, probably about a hundred years old. Again, she was shocked that something very magical had happened to her. And she loved the feeling of being connected spiritually.

Whenever Sheelin would hear these messages, she would follow them, and she would find sea-glass treasures. Taking her first beach trip after her father passed, she heard more instructions, and she discovered a deep turquoise sea-glass heart about two inches across. She was sure that the mermaids were leading her to a gift from her dad, who was a sailor who loved the ocean, as well as a pilot.

Another time, Sheelin's sister was helping her find sea glass on the beach, and they came across an orange sun star, which is a sea star with 20 arms. The creature was more than a foot across, and it was beached on the sand away from the water. It was still alive, and they knew they had to save it. Her sister put a board under the sand and carried the sun star to the sea near the rocks to gently release it. She took about three steps and found a piece of blue sea glass in the shape of a heart. She knew it was her reward for saving the creature.

Sheelin has a friend who owns a house on San Juan Island and another on Kauai. There are beaches

at both houses, and her friend loves to collect sea glass for her. Once, her friend brought Sheelin a ring that had washed up on her Kauai beach. It was a band that appeared to be wrapped in diamonds. Sheelin didn't care if they were real diamonds or not—it was an amazing gift from the sea and her friend. She took it to a jeweler, and he said, "It's real mermaid jewelry!"

The spiritual world has really opened up to Sheelin, and she now understands that she can ask for spiritual connections and talk to the angels or mermaids on a daily basis! Also, after taking my Angel Therapy Practitioner (ATP) course, she has discovered her guides, and has found that her main one is a merman.

During the summertime, Clair Branning spends a lot of time in her hot tub, which she calls her "cold tub" during the summer since she doesn't turn on the heat. She feels so much joy when she spends time there that she gets up as early as possible and does her yoga and meditation right in the tub. The forest that surrounds her yard is filled with birds and

animals happily welcoming the new day. Deer graze out in the distance, and Clair feels instantly at peace.

One morning as she was meditating in the tub, she had the sensation of traveling through a tunnel of light and being transported through time. She saw herself within a human-made pond in the center of a huge temple. Columns stretched out from either side of the pond, and some sort of altar was not far behind her. She was in a pond not much bigger than her eight-seat hot tub, singing and swimming around in small circles. She was a mermaid! As long as she was in the temple pond or other sources of water, she had a mermaid tail. On the land when she was dry, though, she had human legs.

She had beautiful long auburn hair, and many strands of pearls covered her bare breasts. Pearls were draped everywhere around the pond, some even gleaming from the very bottom of it. No wonder Clair had such a desire for pearls this lifetime, owning some 20-odd necklaces and still craving more. These pearls were gifts of affection, given to her as the mermaid guardian of the temple.

As Clair dove down to the bottom of the pond (it was very deep and had a tunnel that ran to the sea itself so that she could come and go as she pleased), she noticed a luscious pearl necklace sinking down

to her from above. She swam up, caught it, and surfaced, laughing with delight.

Sitting at the edge of the pond with his sandaled feet hanging over was her favorite soldier. He was dressed in either Greek or Roman soldier attire. But he looked unhappy and dejected.

"Hi, my love!" he greeted her. She jumped up and kissed him with a giggle. It seemed that she was always laughing and giggling. She was so happy to be alive, here within the temple, honored and appreciated for who she was. Life was good.

"Come out of the pool, please," the soldier said.

"Why, love? I am happy here." And to prove it, she did an especially high backflip, entering the water perfectly, without even the tiniest splash. She resurfaced again and leaned her arms over the lip of the pond, very close to him.

He told her, "Because the old ways are dead. People are talking about you. They will not put up with this much longer. Times have changed."

"But I am the honored guardian of the temple! I am loved. Look at these gifts." And she scooped up an armful of pearls, gold, and other jewels. She cared only for the pearls, though.

"It is what you do . . . for the soldiers . . ."

"I honor them," she replied.

He started pacing around the pond. "It is a sin. Come out of the pool and leave with me today."

"I will not!" she said adamantly and turned her back on him.

She could not understand why he was acting this way. She had honored him, and he had come to love her. She thought back on the bravest and most daring soldiers who would line up to see her, with pearls and gifts in hand. How could this be wrong? It was what had always been, and always would be.

Before he left, the soldier bent over close to her, lifted her chin, and whispered, "Your time is short here. I will return for you." And then he was gone. Her heart felt a slight ache, she loved him so, but displeasure was something that did not stay with her too long. Suddenly she was eager for nightfall, at which time she could walk the streets and go into the marketplace. There were things she wanted to do and see!

Nightfall found her strutting down the cobbled street, and she was a beautiful sight, with her long legs and short tunic adorned with pearls. Her long hair blew slightly in the breeze, and she took a lungful of ocean air and laughed. As she took long, graceful strides, two women passed by, whispering to each other. She smiled and said, "Hail and good

eve to you!" The two women said nothing but continued walking past, shaking their heads and whispering in disapproval. "Tsk, tsk, the things she does in the temple."

Clair stumbled a little, as she felt a sensation she had never experienced before, and didn't even have a name for. But the part of her attached to the present time knew the feeling quite well: shame. She passed a few others, women whispering, men sneering, and some hinting at sexual favors.

Suddenly overwhelmed by the negativity, she fled back to the temple. Crying, and throwing her tunic to the floor, Clair slipped back into the warm comfort of the Mediterranean water, which filled the temple pond.

Then she snapped out of her meditative state, finding herself back in her hot tub in the present day. She said a silent prayer of comfort and healing to her former mermaid self. She wanted to go back in time and hug this innocent, joyful being, but could not. So Clair gave a hug to herself instead.

When Katy's eight-year-old daughter, Mya, was in the shower, she saw the image of two mermaids.

One had blue hair and a blue tail. The other had red hair and a red tail. They began singing a song to her. To Katy, it sounded like high-pitched chanting, and she heard them say hello to her daughter. She also heard the sound of a waterfall. This was the first time she had seen or heard them.

The next time Mya encountered them, she heard them say that they were in the Bermuda Triangle a long, long time ago. A big fairy came and turned them into dolphins so that they would be safe. They began singing a song to her, and it was about peace. They said they *wanted* peace, and *were* peace, and came to talk about joy, love, and peace.

After that, they asked Mya to draw pictures of them on a rock in the water, with the words *love* and *peace* written on the paper. Mya said that the mermaids would be showing themselves to people who wanted to see them.

Katy reported that her daughter had always been open to listening to her intuition, but it seemed to catch her attention more when the family moved to San Diego from Baltimore. Mya grew up always believing she was a dolphin. She requested at a young age to have a dolphin meditation help her get to sleep at night. Little did she know that her middle name was the "call of the dolphin": Bray.

Mya had always wanted to be in water at all times, no matter what kind or what temperature. She just always needed to be around or in it. As such, her move to San Diego seemed to have connected her even more to the beings she felt were "her people."

Now, whenever Mya is in the shower or when the family goes to the beach (which is very often), she gets messages from the mermaids about peace and love. They also love to play with her and talk to her about how they're going to let their presence be known to more and more people.

Avianna's story started when she was a young girl—three years old, to be exact. She had a fascination with water, and loved it as soon as she got in. In fact, it was next to impossible to get her to come out. As she grew and expanded her awareness, she started connecting with her guides and began to understand that her Scorpio sign had much to do with what she was experiencing.

Zoe, her guide, informed her that she had been a mermaid during the time of Atlantis, and that the ocean was her library of information that she could always tap into. Since this discovery, her attraction

to mermaids and water began making more sense, and she started embracing all that she was being shown. Now when Avianna is near water, her intuition expands, the messages multiply, and she often becomes emotional. She also finds that if she's having a rough day, going near water allows her to release the emotions, and she can just let the ocean take it all away in the tide.

Recently during a meditation, Avianna went back into the water, and the mermaids showed her a gold book. She has come to understand that this is her Akashic record, which she will need to access. Her mermaid self along with Spirit is showing her that this spiritual journey is an amazing one, one that needs to be shared with others to create harmony on Earth. She is here to help with this movement. Being a Crystal child, and having once been a mermaid, Avianna knows that her work here is only just beginning!

Kristy M. Ayala has always loved mermaids, as long as she can remember. She loved listening to stories her parents would read to her about mermaids from the children's books that she had as a little girl,

and she would imagine the beautiful world that the mermaids and fish lived in every day.

Kristy wondered what their homes looked like, and if they did all the same things that she did, but under the sea. When she was in the fifth grade, *The Little Mermaid* movie was released in theaters, and she was so excited to see it. She remembers that when the movie began, she felt her heart open up and remembers crying because she was so happy to be connecting with this magical world. Afterward, she began collecting *Little Mermaid* dolls, mugs, sheets, and anything with the character Ariel on it.

Even as she grew into her teenage years, she still secretly loved to dream about life as a mermaid. She had a friend in the neighborhood who had a swimming pool, and whenever she and her friend swam together, they would put brightly colored diving rings around their feet to hold them together. They would then practice swimming like mermaids across the length of the pool. They didn't really know what they were doing, but they just did what they thought a mermaid would do in the water. Thinking about this memory still makes Kristy laugh, because she and her friend had so much fun doing that mermaid swim for hours, back and forth across the pool.

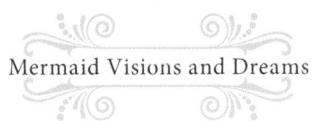

When she went away to college, Kristy took some of her *Little Mermaid* things with her, maybe to help her feel connected to home or to her childhood, and also because she genuinely loved Ariel even though she was an "adult."

During the holiday break her first year in college, *The Little Mermaid* was rereleased in theaters for a very limited time. Kristy's parents called her and asked if she would like to go see it when she came home to visit. She said yes, and they went on opening night. Once again she felt transported to a watery, wonderful world. She realized that even though she was no longer a child, she still had such a deep love for this underwater mermaid world. Her parents told her that they observed her watching the movie and could tell how happy she was, and that it touched their hearts that she was still connected to her childlike self.

Now, all of these years later, it has been such a treat for Kristy to see so many people swimming in the sea with beautiful mermaid tails. She loves watching the videos and looking at photos of amazing real-life mermaids. She feels so much joy and heart expansion when connecting with mermaid energy, and she looks forward to swimming in the same way one day.

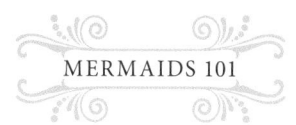

It would appear that this little girl's dream has grown up with her. There is no longer a need for diving rings to bind her feet, as it is now possible to swim in the sea like a mermaid with a real-life mermaid tail. Amazing!

Afterword

Christopher Columbus wrote in his captain's log on his way to North America that a crewman "saw three mermaids, who rose very high from the sea, but they were not as beautiful as they are painted, though to some extent they have a human appearance about the face."

The English astronomer Richard Carrington, who first discovered sunspots in the 1800s, wrote: "In seventeenth century England . . . the existence of mermaids was as firmly established as the existence of shrimps." Mermaids are also referenced in cross-cultural natural-history books from the 1700s and the 1800s. Clearly, the discussion of mermaids is established in our history.

During our lifetime, we have witnessed the extinction of many species. Perhaps future generations will

believe that these now-extinct animals never existed in the first place. Is it possible that in our modern world, so-called mythical creatures such as mermaids and unicorns—who are so widely represented in art and writing cross-culturally—are actually extinct or ascended beings? Perhaps the mermaids' archaeological

DANA RICHARDSON (IN GOLD) AND

IN OUR FAVORITE UNDER

evidence is lost in the oceanic abysses, and the horns of unicorns disintegrated into powder, leaving only skeletal remains that appeared to be ordinary horses.

I believe that the mermaids are making their energetic and spiritual presence known right now, because the waters of Earth need our immediate

ME (IN PINK) ENGAGING

WATER GAME CALLED "TWIRLING."

attention and help. The dolphins, manatees, and whales suffer from slaughter, harassment by Navy sonar noise, pollution, injuries from boats, and the consequences of overfishing. If these issues upset you, then please channel that energy by taking positive corrective action. Write letters, join environmental groups, donate to ocean-related charities, sign petitions, give speeches, and take other action that will aid the ocean. We need your help!

When we hear news accounts of deceased dolphins washing ashore, it's a sign that we need to step up our environmental efforts. We can't afford to allow dolphins to become extinct, and we definitely need to preserve the coral reefs and the overall health of the ocean for our planet's sake.

Perhaps mermaids have returned to the earth to teach humans a better way of relating to the environment and creating sustainable resources. Merpeople are the modern-day Nommos from Sirius, as the Dogon tribe describe their water-based teachers.

Mermaids are very real. *You* are a Merperson in many ways, and it's time for all of us to take charge of our oceans, our planet, and our future. Together, we can swim happily ever after.

About the Author

Doreen Virtue holds B.A., M.A., and Ph.D. degrees in counseling psychology. She has been fascinated by mermaids since she was a little girl, and has written about them in her works *Healing with the Fairies, Angel Medicine, Goddesses & Angels,* and *Magical Mermaids and Dolphins Oracle Cards.* She writes a monthly column for the U.K. magazine *Mermaids & Mythology.* Based in Hawaii, Doreen spends time in the ocean in a swimmable mermaid tail, alongside wild dolphins and her friends who join her in "mermaiding."

Doreen has appeared on *Oprah, CNN, The View,* and other television and radio programs, and writes regular columns for *Woman's World* magazine. Her products are available in most languages worldwide,

on Kindle and other eBook platforms, and as iTunes apps. For more information on Doreen and the workshops she presents, please visit: **www.Angel Therapy.com**. You can listen to Doreen's live weekly radio show, and call her for a reading, by visiting **HayHouseRadio.com**®.

ANGEL THERAPY®

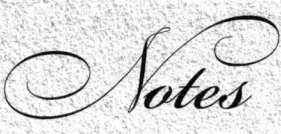

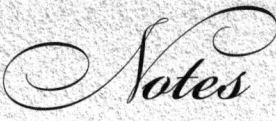

We hope you enjoyed this Hay House Lifestyles book. If you'd like to receive our online catalog featuring additional information on Hay House books and products, or if you'd like to find out more about the Hay Foundation, please contact:

Hay House, Inc., P.O. Box 5100, Carlsbad, CA 92018-5100
(760) 431-7695 or (800) 654-5126
(760) 431-6948 (fax) or (800) 650-5115 (fax)
www.hayhouse.com® • **www.hayfoundation.org**

Published and distributed in Australia by: Hay House Australia Pty. Ltd., 18/36 Ralph St., Alexandria NSW 2015
Phone: 612-9669-4299 • *Fax:* 612-9669-4144
www.hayhouse.com.au

Published and distributed in the United Kingdom by: Hay House UK, Ltd., 292B Kensal Rd., London W10 5BE • *Phone:* 44-20-8962-1230 • *Fax:* 44-20-8962-1239 • www.hayhouse.co.uk

Published and distributed in the Republic of South Africa by: Hay House SA (Pty), Ltd., P.O. Box 990, Witkoppen 2068
Phone/Fax: 27-11-467-8904 • www.hayhouse.co.za

Published in India by: Hay House Publishers India, Muskaan Complex, Plot No. 3, B-2, Vasant Kunj, New Delhi 110 070
Phone: 91-11-4176-1620 • *Fax:* 91-11-4176-1630 • www.hayhouse.co.in

Distributed in Canada by: Raincoast, 9050 Shaughnessy St., Vancouver, B.C. V6P 6E5 • *Phone:* (604) 323-7100
Fax: (604) 323-2600 • www.raincoast.com

Take Your Soul on a Vacation

Visit **www.HealYourLife.com®** to regroup, recharge, and reconnect with your own magnificence.
Featuring blogs, mind-body-spirit news, and life-changing wisdom from Louise Hay and friends.

Visit **www.HealYourLife.com** today!